The Growing Pains of Adrian Mole

Sue Townsend
Retold by Pat McGowan

Burlington Books

The Growing Pains of Adrian Mole

by Sue Townsend
Retold by Pat McGowan

Burlington Books
P. O. Box 54411
3721 Limassol
Cyprus
Burlington Books is an imprint of Danos Books Ltd.
Acknowledgement:
The Growing Pains of Adrian Mole ©1984 Sue Townsend.
First published by Methuen.
Adapted by permission of Curtis Brown Ltd.

The publisher gratefully acknowledges the following for providing photographs: © AP: page 85; © ASAP/Alamy; page 84; © Shutterstock, Inc: pages 26, 39, 57, 59, 86 David Fowler (Margaret Thatcher), 87 Andy Lidstone (Winston Churchill).

The publisher would like to thank the following people:

Castellano:	Elena Terán Herranz
Català:	Natàlia Ros Catalán
Euskara:	Joan Ignazio Bereziartua Iraola
Galego:	Ramón Nicolás Rodríguez

ISBN 978-9963-48-879-7

Burlington Reader No. NB2.01

10 9 8 7 6 5 4 3 2
21 20 19 18 17 16 15 14 13 12

CONTENTS

Introducción

La escritora inglesa Sue Townsend, que nació en la ciudad de Leicester, empezó a escribir en la adolescencia pero no se dedicó a ello profesionalmente hasta los 33 años. En sus trabajos –obras de teatro, musicales y varias novelas– se burla de los aspectos más absurdos del comportamiento humano así como de la vida social y las instituciones británicas.

En este libro descubrirás el mundo de un adolescente inglés de 15 años y su peculiar manera de resolver las dificultades con las que tropieza, sus esfuerzos para adaptarse a los continuos cambios que suponen la llegada inesperada de dos nuevos hermanos, los intentos de reconciliación de sus padres y sus nuevas relaciones amorosas. Si leíste *El diario secreto de Adrian Mole*, ahora puedes continuar disfrutando con sus nuevas aventuras y desventuras.

Introducció

L'escriptora anglesa Sue Townsend que va néixer a la ciutat de Leicester, va començar a escriure durant l'adolescència però no va dedicar-s'hi professionalment fins als 33 anys. En els seus treballs – obres de teatre, musicals i algunes novel·les– se'n riu dels aspectes més absurds del comportament humà, així com de la vida social i les institucions britàniques.

En aquest llibre descobriràs el món d'un adolescent anglès de 15 anys i la seva peculiar manera de resoldre les dificultats amb què ensopega, els seus esforços per adaptar-se als canvis continus que suposen l'arribada inesperada de dos nous germans, els intents de reconciliació dels seus pares i les seves noves relacions amoroses. Si vas llegir *El diari secret d'Adrian Mole*, ara pots continuar gaudint amb les seves noves aventures i desventures.

Sarrera

Sue Townsend idazle ingelesa, Leicester hirian jaioa, gaztaroan hasi zen idazten, baina ez zuen horretan profesionalki jardun 33 urte izan zituen arte. Bere lanetan –teatroko obrak, musikazkoak eta hainbat eleberri– giza jokabidearen alderdirik zentzugabeenez trufatzen da, bai eta Britainia Handiko gizarteko bizitzaz eta instituzioez ere.

Liburu honetan, 15 urteko gazte ingeles baten munduaren berri jakingo duzu: zein modu berezian ebazten dituen bidean topatzen dituen zailtasunak, nolako ahaleginak egiten dituen bi senide berriren etorrera ezustekoak dakarzkion aldaketa etengabekoetara moldatzeko, nola saiatzen diren gurasoak adiskidetzen, eta zer amodiozko harreman berriak dituzten. *Adrian Moleren egunkari ezkutua* irakurri bazenuen, orain ere gozatuz jarrai dezakezu haren abentura eta zorigaitz berriekin.

Limiar

A escritora inglesa Sue Townsend, que naceu na cidade de Leicester, comezou a escribir na adolescencia aínda que non se dedicase a iso profesionalmente até os 33 anos. Nos seus traballos – obras de teatro, musicais e varias novelas– búrlase dos aspectos máis absurdos do comportamento humano así coma da vida social e as institucións británicas.

Neste libro descubrirás o mundo dun adolescente inglés de 15 anos e o seu peculiar xeito de resolver os atrancos cos que tropeza, os seus esforzos para se adaptar ás continuas mudanzas que supoñen a chegada inesperábel de dous novos irmáns, os intentos de reconciliación dos seus pais e as súas novas relacións amorosas. Se liches *O diario secreto de Adrian Mole*, agora podes continuar gozando coas súas novas aventuras e desventuras.

THE CHARACTERS

PRE-READING ACTIVITIES

1 Read the sentences from letters to an advice column and complete them with a suitable word or expression below.

embarrass *nervous breakdown* *worry* *shocked*
pregnant *only child* *divorce* *get on well*

1. My parents always .... me in front of my friends.
2. My parents are getting a .... and I have to decide who to live with.
3. I hate sharing a room with my sister. I wish I were an ....
4. My brother and I don't .... We're always fighting.
5. My girlfriend thinks she might be .... We're too young to be parents.
6. My biggest .... is that I will fail my exam. I need to do well.
7. I'm .... My father is having an affair. I don't think my mother knows anything.
8. If I don't get any privacy at home, I will have a ....

2 *Growing pains* are pains in the muscles as a result of rapid growth. *Growing pains* is also an expression that describes the emotional difficulties during adolescence. Look at some typical adolescent issues below and match each one to a suitable quote.

a. brother / sister rivalry
b. body image
c. dating
d. social acceptance
e. exam anxiety
f. generation gap

.... 1. "I'm terrified of failing maths this year."
.... 2. "My parents give my brother whatever he wants. It's not fair."
.... 3. "How can I go out looking like this? I've got spots all over my face."
.... 4. "My girlfriend wants me to spend all my time with her but what about my friends?"
.... 5. "My parents are so old fashioned. They don't understand anything."
.... 6. "I want those new jeans because everyone is wearing them."

CHAPTER 1

April

Last night I made a model aeroplane but my nose stuck to the plane.

Sunday, April 4th 1982.

Last night I made a model aeroplane and decided to try an experimental sniff of glue but my nose stuck to the plane. My father took me to hospital to have the plane removed. Today my nose is **swollen** and really hurts. It's so bad that I'm very worried that it might explode and take my brain with it! I phoned the hospital and spoke to the nurse. She said that I was probably allergic to the glue and that my nose would be better in a few days. She added, "Perhaps it will teach you not to sniff glue again." I tried to explain but she put the phone down.

Pandora came to visit me but I didn't want to see her. She wouldn't like me any more if she saw my horrible nose!

Monday, April 5th.

Just my luck! It's the first day of the school holidays and I can't go out because of my huge, swollen nose. Even my mother is worried about it now. She wanted to **prick** it with a sterilised needle, but I wouldn't let her. She has no idea how to **sew**.

Our dog is in love with a pedigree dog called Mitzi. I tried to explain to the dog that it had no chance of success, but it didn't understand. Being in love is no joke. I have the same problem with Pandora that the dog has with Mitzi. We are both in a lower social class than our loved ones.

Thursday, April 8th.

My nose is a little better. I allowed Pandora to visit me in my dark bedroom. We kissed a lot. I wanted more, but Pandora said we must wait until we have passed our exams. All this sexual frustration isn't good for me. I've got 38 spots.

Friday, April 9th.

Barry Kent* has been telling everybody that I'm addicted to glue. His aunt's a cleaner in the hospital and heard about the model aeroplane incident. I think it's terrible that cleaners are allowed to talk about people's private medical secrets. They should take the Hippocratic oath** like doctors and nurses.

My mother's depressed. She sits in the house, smoking and watching TV. I don't know why she's depressed. My father doesn't know either.

Monday, April 12th.

My mother's acting more strangely than usual. Today she dropped cigarette ash on my sheets while she was changing them. When I objected, she said, "Oh, Adrian, why can't you be untidy like *normal* teenagers?"

My mother and father are always arguing about their bedroom. My father's side of the room is always tidy, but my mother's side is terrible. I **pity** my father having to share a room with her.

Tuesday, April 13th.

I asked my father why he had married my mother. He explained that he met my mother when miniskirts were in fashion. In those days my mother had good legs, whereas most women looked terrible in miniskirts. I was shocked and told him that I loved Pandora because she was intelligent and compassionate. My father just laughed.

* *an unpleasant boy in Adrian's class*

** *a doctor's promise of confidentiality about a patient's illness*

Wednesday, April 14th.

Mitzi's owner came and asked my mother to keep our dog away from Mitzi. My mother said that our dog lived in a liberal home and could go where it wanted. Mitzi's owner **threatened to report** our dog to the police. My mother laughed and said, "Why don't you take us all down to the police station right now?"

Thursday, April 15th.

Woke up at 4 a.m. with toothache. Took six junior aspirins for the pain. At 5 a.m. I woke my parents up and told them that I was in agony. My father said, "It's your own fault. You didn't go to your last three dentist's appointments."

At 5.30 a.m. I asked my father to take me to hospital, but he wouldn't. It's OK for him; he hasn't got any real teeth. I promised myself that from now on I would go to the dentist four times a year, even if I wasn't in pain.

At 9 a.m. my mother woke me and told me that she had made an emergency appointment for me with the dentist. I informed her that the pain had stopped and told her to cancel the appointment.

Friday, April 16th.

Woke up at 3 a.m. with terrible toothache. I tried to suffer in silence, but my father must have heard me crying because he came and told me to be quiet. He had to work the next day and needed his sleep. On the way back to his bedroom, he **slipped** on one of my mother's magazines lying on the floor and she woke up. Then the dog started barking. Once again, I got no sleep.

Saturday, April 17th.

I'm still in bed with toothache. I've phoned Pandora. She's coming to see me tomorrow. I told her to bring me a Mars bar.

"To make your teeth even better?" she said, sarcastically.

The dog's still in love with Mitzi. It isn't eating.

Sunday, April 18th.

Pandora has just left my bedroom. I'm so frustrated. I can't go on like this. I've written to Aunt Clara's Problem Page about my problem.

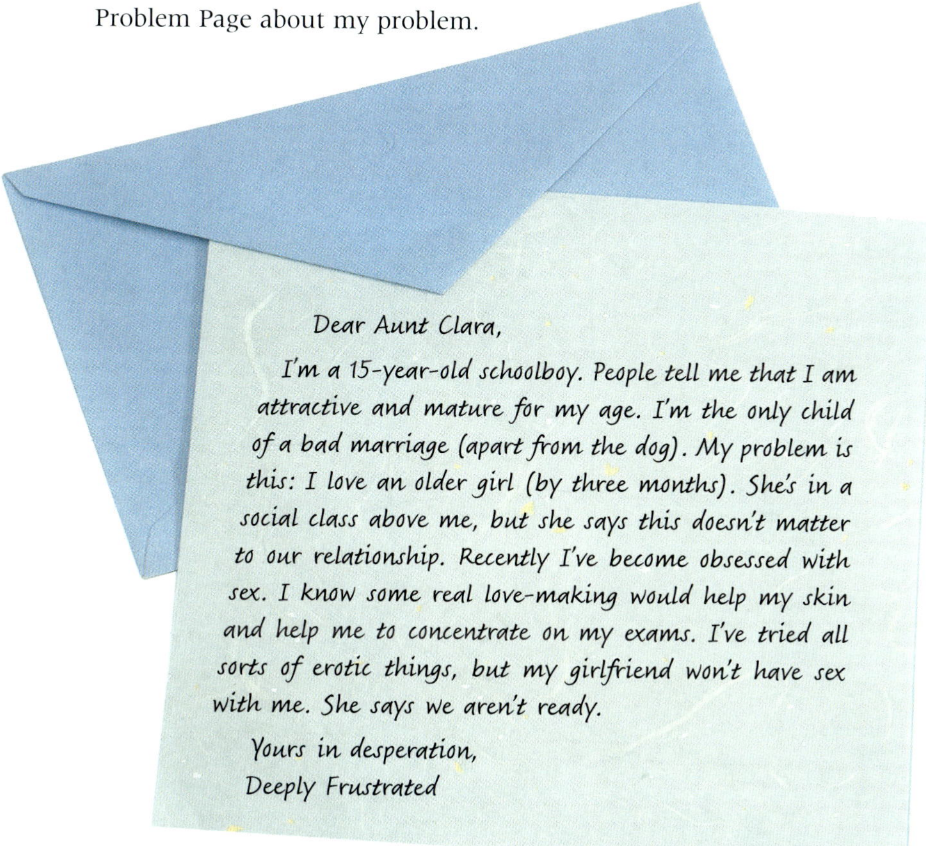

Dear Aunt Clara,

I'm a 15-year-old schoolboy. People tell me that I am attractive and mature for my age. I'm the only child of a bad marriage (apart from the dog). My problem is this: I love an older girl (by three months). She's in a social class above me, but she says this doesn't matter to our relationship. Recently I've become obsessed with sex. I know some real love-making would help my skin and help me to concentrate on my exams. I've tried all sorts of erotic things, but my girlfriend won't have sex with me. She says we aren't ready.

Yours in desperation,
Deeply Frustrated

Monday, April 19th.

I'm now minus a front tooth! The stupid dentist took it out instead of repairing it. He even put it in a piece of paper and gave it to me to take home! He told me he had often seen me walking home from school eating a Mars bar, and it would be my own fault if I had no teeth at 30.

I will walk home another way in future.

Tuesday, April 20th.

My mother's furious with the dentist. I look like a mass murderer. She's written him a letter insisting that he make a false tooth for free.

School was terrible. Everyone **called me names**. Even Pandora was a little distant.

My mother was furious with the dentist. I look like a mass murderer.

Thursday, April 22nd.

I didn't want to go to school this morning, so I stayed in bed till 12.45 p.m. I asked my mother for a note to give my teacher. She wrote, "Adrian didn't come to school this morning because he didn't get up until 12.45." The teacher was very angry but said, "At least your mother's honest. Most parents aren't." I'll ask my father to write my notes in future. He lies easily.

Monday, April 26th.

I heard a mysterious conversation today. My mother said, "George, it's positive." My father said, "Oh no, I can't get up at 3 a.m., not at my age." I think my mother is making unreasonable sexual demands on my father.

I received a reply from Aunt Clara. She told me that sex was only a small part of life and that I should enjoy my teenage years. Enjoy my teenage years! They're full of problems! I can't wait to be an adult.

Wednesday, April 28th.

Stick Insect (Doreen Slater)* came to our house today. She opened her coat (she looks quite fat now) and said, "I thought you ought to know, George." Then she left. I didn't tell my mother when she came home. She gets very angry if anyone mentions Stick Insect's name.

CHAPTER 2

May and June

Sunday, May 2nd.

Nigel told me his parents want to emigrate to Australia. I was amazed! How can any English person want to live abroad? Nigel agrees. He asked me if he could stay and live with us.

Wednesday, May 5th.

We got a strange phone call today. I answered the phone, but before I could speak, a woman's voice said, "Mrs Mole? This is the clinic. You have an appointment with us on Friday at 2 p.m. You'll get professional help for your problem. Please be punctual." Then she put the phone down.

What does it all mean? My mother hasn't said that she's ill. What problem does she have? Which clinic is it?

* *Adrian's father's girlfriend when he was separated from his wife*

Monday, May 10th.

We learned about diabetes in Biology today. The teacher explained how to **measure** our blood sugar level. I suddenly remembered that I'd forgotten to tell my mother about her appointment at the clinic. It probably wasn't important.

I asked Pandora to show me one of her **breasts**, but she wouldn't. I tried to explain that I wanted to get more experience of life, but she just buttoned her jacket and went home.

Thursday, May 13th.

I received a letter from Pandora this morning. She wants to end our relationship. She says I'm obsessed with her body and that I should get psychiatric help.

Before I opened that letter, I was a normal kind of intellectual teenager. I'm now an adult and I'm suffering. I'm no longer young. I wouldn't be surprised if my hair has started to turn grey.

I'm in torment! I love her! I love her! Oh God! Oh Pandora!

3 a.m. I've used a whole roll of toilet paper to dry my tears.

5 a.m. I didn't sleep well. The world's no longer exciting and colourful. It's grey and sad. I thought of killing myself, but my mother would be shocked if she came into my room and found my dead body.

Saturday, May 15th.

Why did I ask Pandora to show me her breast? I could have asked anybody. Nigel says that Sharon Botts will show everything for 50p and a kilo of grapes.

I've written Pandora a short letter to say sorry. I'll deliver it by hand after dark.

10 p.m. There were a lot of visitors at Pandora's house and expensive cars in the driveway. At first I thought it was a funeral because I saw a vicar, but then a cowboy and a monster walked past. It was a fancy dress party. I hid behind a tree so that I could see better. A gorilla started dancing with a **belly dancer** who was wearing a **yashmak** and a costume that showed most of her breasts.

I couldn't see Pandora anywhere, so I ran to the door and put the letter in the letterbox.

When I got home I found Queen Victoria and Prince Albert in the kitchen. Queen Victoria said, "We're going to the Braithwaites' party." Nobody tells me anything in this house.

Monday, May 17th.

I was in the school cloakroom doing my homework when I heard Pandora talking to Claire Neilson. "I'm rather worried. I enjoyed dressing up as a belly dancer so much, even though it's against my feminist principles." So, Pandora, who wouldn't show me *one* of her breasts in the privacy of my bedroom, is happy to show *both* of them in public!!!

Tuesday, May 18th.

I met Stick Insect in the library. She looked very fat. We talked about the time when she had been my father's girlfriend. I said it was better for her without him. She said, "He's a different person when he's with me. He's so sweet and kind." She used the present tense when she talked about my father. It's terrible that a woman of 30 doesn't know basic grammar!

Wednesday, May 19th.

No word from Pandora. She ignores me when we meet at school. I've asked Nigel where I can find Sharon Botts. I also went to the shop to find out how much a kilo of grapes costs.

While I was listening to the radio, my mother asked me if I liked being an only child. I said that I preferred it.

Saturday, May 22nd.

My father's just asked me if I would like a sister or a brother. I said neither. Why do they keep on talking about children? I hope they're not going to adopt one. They're terrible parents. Look at me, I'm completely neurotic.

Sunday, May 23rd.

I couldn't sleep, so I got up very early and went for a walk past Pandora's house. I thought of her lying in her bed and tears came to my eyes. But I wiped my eyes and went to see old Bert and Queenie.* They were still in bed, so I went home, made two cups of tea and took them to my parents. They weren't even grateful. My mother told me to go away and buy the papers or something. I bought the papers, read them and took them to my parents. I think the central **heating** is too hot because their faces were very red. As I went out of the room, I heard my mother say, "George, we must get a lock on that door."

Wednesday, May 26th.

My mother is pregnant. My mother!!!!!!

How can she do this to me? Everyone will laugh at me at school. In November a baby will be living in this house. I hope they don't expect me to share a room with it.

10 p.m. I kissed my poor mother goodnight. She said, "Are you pleased about the baby, Adrian?" I lied and said, "Yes."

What about my exams? How can I study with a screaming baby in the house?

How can I study with a screaming baby in the house?

---

* *an old man and his wife whom Adrian visits and helps*

Tuesday, June 1st.

Pandora hasn't spoken to me for 22 days.

What have my mother, Mitzi the dog and Claire Neilson's cat got in common? They're all pregnant!

Monday, June 7th.

Stick Insect's also pregnant! I saw her in the supermarket this afternoon. I wonder who the father is.

Tuesday, June 15th.

We've got a new postman. He's called Courtney Elliot. He's no ordinary postman. He wears a smart shirt and a red bow tie with his grey uniform. It seems he was a university professor who didn't like academic life. He immediately made friends with the dog. He gave my father a letter and said, "From the **tax department**, I'm afraid, Mr Mole." The tax department had learned that my father was doing business from home and asked him to fill in a form. My father said, "Somebody hates me and has told the tax department about me!" My parents counted how many enemies they had. There were 27, not including relatives.

Stick Insect has walked past our house six times.

Monday, June 21st.

The headmaster announced to the whole school this morning that Prince William had been born. Claire Neilson shouted, "How much did he weigh?" Pandora shouted, "How much will he cost?" The headmaster told her to leave the assembly hall. Poor Pandora, her face was red. When she passed, I smiled at her, but she ignored me.

Wednesday, June 23rd.

Pandora's being **punished** at school. She has to sit and work on her own. I left a note for her on her coat in the cloakroom:

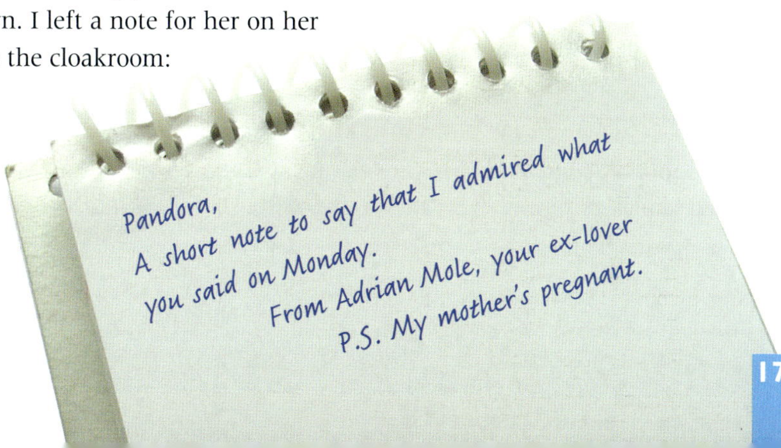

Thursday, June 24th.

I found a note on my coat this morning.

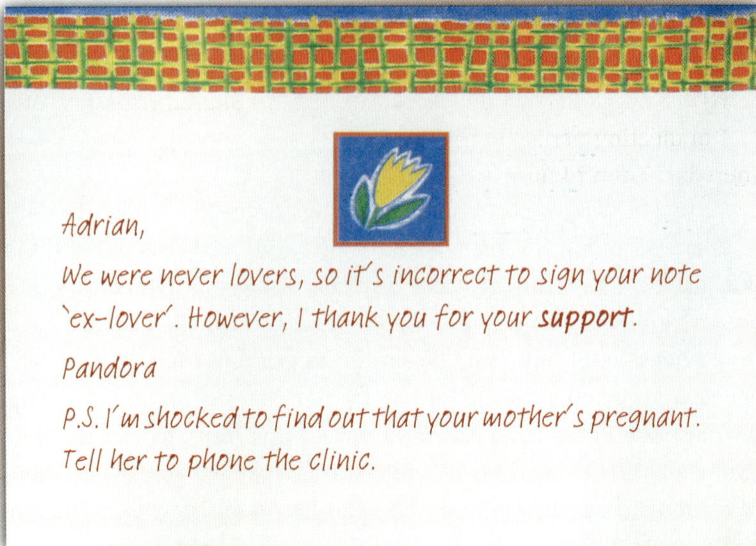

Adrian,

We were never lovers, so it's incorrect to sign your note 'ex-lover'. However, I thank you for your **support**.

Pandora

P.S. I'm shocked to find out that your mother's pregnant. Tell her to phone the clinic.

My 'thing' is normally 3 cm long and 14 cm when extended. I'm very worried. Nigel says his thing is much longer, and he's only a week older than me.

Monday, June 28th.

We had the usual last-minute discussion about where we're going for our summer holiday. My father said, "It'll probably be our last. This time next year we'll have the baby." My mother got angry and said that having a baby wasn't going to limit her activities and that if she wanted to go walking in India next year, she would put the baby on her back and go. Walking in India! She complains if she has to walk to the bus stop!

I suggested the Lake District. My father suggested Skegness. My mother suggested Greece. Nobody could agree, so we each wrote our choice on a piece of paper and put the papers into a tin. Skegness won. Too bad!

Wednesday, June 30th.

My mother wants to move house. She wants to sell the house that I've lived in all my life. She said we'll need more room for the baby. How stupid can she be? Babies hardly take any space at all. They are only about 50 cm long.

Nigel's organised a **blind date** for me with Sharon Botts.

I'm meeting her at the **roller-skating rink** on Saturday. I'm very nervous. I don't know how to roller-skate – or make love.

CHAPTER 3

July

Friday, July 2nd.

I borrowed Nigel's roller-skates and practised on the pavement. I'm OK as long as I've got something to hold on to. I wanted to wear my skates in the house so that I would develop confidence, but my father complained about damaging the kitchen floor.

Saturday, July 3rd.

12.15 p.m. Got up at 6 a.m. for more roller-skating practice, but our neighbour, Mr Davis, shouted at me because I was making a noise so early in the morning, so I had to stop. Bought a kilo of grapes when the shop opened. Came home, had a bath, washed my hair and cut my toenails. Then I put all my clothes on the bed and tried to decide what to wear. Finally, at 10.30, I phoned Nigel and asked him what youths wore at roller-skating rinks. He said, "They wear red satin running shorts, sleeveless satin vests, white knee socks, Sony Walkman earphones and one gold earring." I finally chose my black gym shorts, my white **string vest** and my grey knee socks. I'm the only person in the world who doesn't have a Sony Walkman and I haven't had my ears pierced, but I hope Sharon Botts won't mind too much.

6 p.m. That's the first and last time I go roller-skating. Sharon Botts is an expert. She skates at 60 km/h. She sometimes slowed down and said, "Stop holding the barrier, idiot!"

We went to the coffee bar and had a Coke and I gave her the grapes. She said, "Why have you brought me grapes? I'm not ill." I tried to make it clear by looking at her lycra body stocking and miniskirt, but then the roller disco started and she went to dance. She was soon surrounded by tall youths in satin shorts, so I went home.

I phoned Nigel and told him that Sharon Botts was a waste of time. He said that Sharon had already phoned him and told him that I'd **embarrassed** her by wearing my gym shorts. Nigel said that he's not going to organise any more blind dates.

Sunday, July 4th.

Bert Baxter phoned at 1 p.m. and asked me to go urgently to his house. When I arrived, the TV was off, so I knew something serious had happened. He said, "Queenie doesn't feel well. I asked her what was wrong and she said, 'I've got terrible pains in my chest.' " Bert hadn't phoned the doctor because Queenie was frightened of doctors. I phoned my mother and asked for advice. She said she would come immediately. While we were waiting, I made a cup of tea, fed the dog and made Bert a **beetroot** sandwich.

My parents came and my mother phoned for an ambulance. When it arrived, she went with Queenie to the hospital, and my father and I stayed with Bert. Two hours later my mother phoned to say that Queenie had had a **stroke** and would be in hospital for a long time. Bert said, "What am I going to do without my girl to help me?" Girl! Queenie is 78.

Monday, July 5th.

Queenie can't speak – she can't move the muscles of her mouth. My mother's been at Bert's all day, cleaning and cooking. My father's going to go and see him every day after work. I've promised to take Bert's horrible dog, Sabre, for his morning and evening walks.

I left a note on Pandora's coat today. I told her about Queenie and suggested that she visit Bert, as he's very sad.

Friday, July 9th.

The summer holidays started today – no more school for eight weeks. Then tonight, something even *better* happened. I was at Bert's house, ironing his enormous underpants when Pandora walked into the living room. Bert looked much happier and told me to make some tea. I looked **longingly** at Pandora and she looked longingly back at me!!!!!!

I was ironing Bert's enormous underpants when Pandora walked into the living room.

At 9.30 p.m. I washed Bert and then helped him to get into bed. When he started snoring, Pandora and I fell into each other's arms. We stayed like that till 10 p.m. On the way home I asked Pandora when she had realised that she still loved me. She said, "When I saw you ironing those horrible underpants."

Monday, July 12th.

I have been round to Bert's every day to take horrible Sabre out for a walk. I hate the way people cross the road when they see us coming. I hope Queenie gets better soon; she loves to be seen with Sabre.

Thursday, July 15th.

Pandora's parents took Bert to the hospital to visit Queenie this evening, so Pandora and I spent two brilliant hours lying on her parents' bed watching a video. I was very careful not to touch Pandora's erotic zones. When the film finished, we talked about our futures. Pandora said that after university, she would like to go and help people in the Third World countries.

Unfortunately, the cigarette she was smoking fell out of her hand and burned a hole in the bed. Pandora's very worried; her parents don't smoke.

Friday, July 16th.

Stick Insect has just phoned to ask if my father's home from work yet. Her voice sounded sad. I expect she's **regretting** her promiscuous behaviour now that her baby's about to be born. I told my mother it was a wrong number. It's not good for pregnant women to worry about things like that.

Saturday, July 17th.

I've just seen my father and Stick Insect walking arm in arm. It's good of my father to help Stick Insect, but he should be more careful of public opinion. If people see a man arm in arm with a pregnant woman, they'll think he's the baby's father.

Monday, July 19th.

Went to see Grandma. She was making her Christmas cake. I helped her make the cake and I made a wish while I put the 20 pence coins in. I was very selfish. I could have wished for world peace or for Queenie to get better quickly, but instead I wished that the spots on my shoulders would disappear before my summer holiday. I hate the thought of all the holiday-makers on Skegness beach seeing all my spots.

Wednesday, July 21st.

My father announced at breakfast that he's going to have a vasectomy. I couldn't eat my sausages after that.

Only 10 days to go before our holiday in Skegness begins. I've asked my father if Pandora can come with us. The thought of being alone with my parents for two weeks is depressing. My father said, "She's welcome to come if she pays the cost of £120."

Thursday, July 22nd.

While we were cleaning Bert's house, I asked Pandora if she would like to come to Skegness. She said, "Darling, I would follow you to hell, but I won't go to Skegness." Bert was very angry and told her she was a snob. Pandora's face went red. She said, "I'm very sorry, Bert. People forget so easily that they're privileged."

To change the subject, Pandora phoned the hospital and asked how Queenie was. The nurse said that Queenie had asked for her lipstick today. Bert smiled when he heard the news. "That's good," he said. "That means that Queenie's getting better."

We put Bert to bed, then I walked Pandora home. We had a long, passionate kiss, then Pandora whispered, "Adrian, take me to Skegness." It was the most romantic sentence I've ever heard.

Saturday, July 24th.

I went shopping for holiday clothes today. My mother came with me. We had an argument about my taste in clothes. Quite a few teenagers in the shop were having arguments with their parents. My mother and I didn't speak for some time, until she tried to make me buy a yellow leopard-skin T-shirt. I told her I wouldn't try it on, so she bought it for herself! The shop assistant said, "You've got a **cool** mother."

Monday, July 26th.

Courtney Elliot, the postman, brought my father a letter this morning from his boss, telling him that he wasn't working fast enough. My father was very angry but my mother said, "He's right, George, you're always home early." My father went out and **slammed the door**. My mother made Courtney a cup of tea and I went to see Bert.

My mother tried to make me buy a yellow leopard-skin T-shirt.

Tuesday, July 27th.

Pandora's father won't give her £120 for Skegness! He said he'd already paid £400 for a canoeing holiday for his family in September. So, there will be two weeks without Pandora, unless I can find a way to earn £120 quickly. Pandora doesn't have any money of her own; she spends all her money buying strings for her viola.

My mother's **bump** is getting bigger every day. She seems quite *proud* of it. She's showing it to everybody who comes to the house. I have to leave the room.

Thursday, July 29th.

My father has been working very hard for the last three days. He hasn't been coming home till 10 p.m. He's getting very worried about leaving his work to go on holiday.

We went to see Queenie in hospital. She can't speak properly, so it was embarrassing trying to understand what she was saying. I left after 20 minutes, tired from smiling.

Friday, July 30th.

Our family went to Pandora's house to discuss what her family will have to do to look after Bert while we're on holiday. My mother gave Pandora's mother a long list. The last thing on it was 'The Best of Luck!'

Saturday, July 31st. Rio Grande Boarding House*

Pandora came round this morning to say goodbye, but I was too busy packing and looking for my swimming costume to feel sad. We finally left at 6 p.m.; the car **broke down** on the way, so we didn't arrive at the Rio Grande until 12.30. It was locked. We rang the doorbell for ages, and finally a miserable-looking man unlocked the door. He said, "Mole family? You're late. These doors are locked at 11 p.m. and there's a 50p **fine** for latecomers. I'm Bernard Porke, the owner."

Now I'm in my basement room. I wish I were at home.

* *a private house where the owner provides rooms and food for people on holiday in exchange for payment*

CHAPTERS 1-3 ACTIVITIES

1 Have the words below got positive or negative meanings? Write each word in the correct mirror.

unreasonable grateful depressed lie confidence tidy smart pain pleased miserable selfish immature success

2 The words in bold are in the wrong sentences. Write each word in the correct sentence.

1. There's a lot of food, would you like to **ignore** it with me? ....
2. Can I **damage** your pen? I left mine at home. ....
3. Please **look after** what he said. He didn't mean it. ....
4. I need a job because I want to **share** some money. ....
5. My parents are going out so I have to **earn** my little sister. ....
6. Could you **wonder** when the guests are arriving? ....
7. I **borrow** where he is. He should have been home by now. ....
8. Be careful not to **find out** anything in the shop. ....

3 Match each sentence beginning to the correct ending?

1. Adrian wrote to Aunt Clara because
2. Adrian thought he looked like a mass murderer because
3. Pandora wanted to end her relationship with Adrian because
4. The Moles put papers into a tin because
5. Pandora's father wouldn't pay for her to go to Skegness because
6. In Skegness, Adrian wanted to go home because

.... a. they couldn't agree on a holiday destination.
.... b. Bernard Porke was very unpleasant.
.... c. they were going away in September.
.... d. he was sexually frustrated.
.... e. he was obsessed with her body.
.... f. the dentist took out his tooth.

4 Answer the questions. Write the answers in your notebook.

1. What happened to Adrian's nose?
2. What difference is there between Adrian's father's reason for marrying his mother and Adrian's reason for loving Pandora?
3. Why were 'Queen Victoria' and 'Prince Albert' in Adrian's kitchen?
4. What three indications was Adrian given that his mother was pregnant?
5. Bert phoned Adrian when Queenie didn't feel well. What does this tell you about the relationship between Bert and Adrian?
6. The people around Adrian were very helpful to Bert. What are some examples of their kindness?

Did You know?

Mary Quant was a young British designer who sold clothes that reflected the British youth in the 1960s. When she designed skirts that were several inches above the knee, the miniskirt was born. She named it after her favourite car, the Mini, and it became an instant success.

CHAPTER 4

August

Sunday, August 1st.

I was woken up by Mr Porke shouting, "Only one piece of bacon per plate, Beryl! Are you trying to ruin me?" I got dressed quickly and ran up the stairs to my parents' room. My father told me to run down to the dining room and get a good table.

Everybody in the dining room was whispering. My mother never whispers, so everybody, including Mr Porke, heard her complaining about the uncomfortable beds. I'm sure that's why our table only got two pieces of fried bread.

I was woken up by Mr Porke shouting.

Wednesday, August 4th.

The sun shone today! It was very hot, but I've got 18 spots on my shoulders, so I couldn't take my shirt off.

I sent Pandora a donkey postcard. I wrote, "The sun is shining today, but it can't end the black despair caused by our separation. It's a cultural desert here."

Tuesday, August 10th.

During the evening meal, Mr Porke brought my father a message that a good friend had been taken into the Royal Hospital and would he please phone the hospital immediately. It was a mystery to all of us. My father hasn't got any good friends. He left the table in a panic and was away for about 15 minutes. When he came back, he said, "I've got something to tell you both. Let's go somewhere private."

We sat on the beach and he told us he was the father of Stick Insect's one-day-old baby boy. About 60 hours passed. Then my mother said, "What's his name?" My father said, "Brett." I couldn't think of anything to say, so I said nothing. I still can't think of anything to say, so I'm going to sleep.

Wednesday, August 11th.

12.30 p.m. My father has gone to see Stick Insect and the baby. My mother made him go. I can't think of anything to say to my mother. She just sits in her room with her hands over her bump. She hasn't cried once. I'm very worried.

5 p.m. I phoned Mrs Braithwaite, Pandora's mother, and told her everything. She was very **sympathetic**. She said she would come to Skegness and collect us.

I packed all the suitcases and made my mother wash her face and do her hair. Then we sat and waited for Mrs Braithwaite.

Thursday, August 12th. Home

As soon as she saw Mrs Braithwaite, my mother started to cry. Mrs Braithwaite said, "Men are all the same, Pauline." We got home at 4.30 this morning. Mrs Braithwaite doesn't like driving over 50 km/h, so it took us five hours to travel the 240 kilometres from Skegness home. I went straight to bed. I didn't want to check if my father was in his room.

Friday, August 13th.

My father's **razor** wasn't in the bathroom, so I had to use my mother's pink underarm one. I had to shave and look my best, because Grandma was coming and we were going to tell her the terrible news that her son had an illegitimate child, while his wife was expecting a legitimate one.

Saturday, August 14th.

Grandma's changed sides! She's given some of *our* baby clothes to Stick Insect's baby boy. I know Grandma doesn't like my mother, but at least my mother is my father's legal wife.

My father came and asked if he could come home. I wanted my mother to say yes, but she said no. So my father's gone to live with Grandma. He's taken the stereo with him.

Monday, August 16th.

Pandora shocked me today. She asked me if I was curious about my brother, Brett. It's strange to think I've got a brother. I hope he has better luck with his skin than me.

A cheque for £50 arrived from my father. My mother **tore it up** and sent the pieces back to my father. How stupid can you be? My mother regretted it later.

Stick Insect, her other son, Maxwell, and Brett have moved into Grandma's house.

My mother tore the cheque up and sent the pieces back to my father.

Wednesday, August 18th.

Took the dog for a walk, went to Grandma's and looked casually into Brett's **pram**. He's got lots of wrinkles. I didn't see Stick Insect or my father. I didn't tell my mother.

I'm not interested in sex any more. It seems to cause a lot of trouble.

Friday, August 20th.

My mother's too depressed to do any cooking, so I have to do it. **So far** we've had salad with tuna or cold meat, but I think I'll try something different tomorrow – salad with ham, perhaps.

My father keeps phoning to see how my mother is. Today he asked me if she'd mentioned divorce. I said no, but that she looked as if she was thinking about it.

Saturday, August 21st.

Went to Grandma's again. Brett's got my father's big nose. Grandma was changing his dirty **nappy**. I was amazed at how big his thing is. My father and Stick Insect were out buying baby equipment.

Friday, August 27th.

My mother's made an appointment to see the bank manager. She wants to borrow some money because she hasn't got any left. I hope they lend her the money. I haven't had any pocket money for two weeks.

Saturday, August 28th.

Pandora is taking canoeing lessons to prepare for her holiday. She had her first lesson today. She invited me to come and watch and, if necessary, give her the kiss of life if she fell out and nearly **drowned**. She looked very erotic in her wetsuit and crash helmet. For the first time in ages I felt my thing moving on its own.

Tuesday, August 31st.

My mother went to see the bank manager this morning. The manager knew my mother wasn't working and that she only got money from the Social Security, so he wouldn't lend her the money. I'll have to get a Saturday job, because I need money desperately. I've got two months of library fines to pay.

CHAPTER 5

September

Wednesday, September 1st.

Pandora took a canoeing test this afternoon. She passed the test easily. Her instructor has offered to prepare her for her next test.

Pandora has asked me to join her in her new hobby, but I'm scared of drowning. I'm quite happy sitting by the river thinking my intellectual thoughts and holding Pandora's towel.

Friday, September 3rd.

It is now very obvious that my mother is pregnant. She sticks out in front and walks in a strange way. She finds it difficult to **bend down**, so I spend a lot of time picking things up for her.

Pandora and her parents are going on holiday tomorrow. I've offered to feed their cat. They've accepted my kind offer and have given me their keys. It's a huge responsibility. Their house is full of expensive electrical appliances and antiques.

Saturday, September 4th.

I waved goodbye to my love today. She blew kisses from the back window of the Volvo and then disappeared. I waited half an hour (in case they'd forgotten something), then went into the house, made myself a cup of tea and a tuna sandwich and sat down to watch their big colour TV. (I must remember to replace the tuna before they come back.)

Monday, September 6th.

I spent all morning watering the Braithwaites' plants. It can't be healthy living among so many plants. It's amazing that Pandora and her parents don't die of oxygen starvation.

I realised with horror that school starts next Monday and I've only spent one day studying for my exams. Took my history books to the Braithwaites' study. I thought the studious atmosphere might help, but I still can't remember the dates of battles or Archduke Ferdinand's middle name.

Thursday, September 9th.

Went to Bert Baxter's house to tidy up. Queenie is coming home from hospital on Saturday.

Received a letter from Pandora today. She nearly drowned while canoeing! She didn't seem at all worried. I felt ill after reading her letter. I had to take an aspirin and lie down.

Sunday, September 12th.

Pandora came home today!

Ironed my school uniform. It's much too small for me, but my mother hasn't got enough money to buy a new one.

Monday, September 13th.

I'm now a fifth-year pupil and I've got the privilege of using the side entrance of the school. I can't wait until next year when I'll be allowed to use the *front* entrance. Perhaps I'm perverted, but I really enjoyed watching the younger pupils pushing through the entrance at the back of the school.

Had my English exam. Was the first to finish. It was easy.

Tuesday, September 14th.

I've got a new teacher. His name is Mr Lambert. He likes being friendly. He said, "Consider me a friend. I want to hear any problems you've got at school or at home." I've made an appointment to see him after school tomorrow.

My mother is 38 today. I bought her a card which said, 'Happy 18th Birthday', but I cleverly changed the '1' into a '3' by using Tipp-ex. My father sent her a card with a sad cat on it. Inside he had written, 'Yours as ever, George.' Horrible Lucas* sent a card too. Inside he had written, 'Pauline, I'll never forget that night in the woods. Yours with all my love, Bimbo.' She had 10 other cards, all from women.

Wednesday, September 15th.

My father phoned before I went to school this morning. He wanted to speak to my mother, but she wouldn't talk to him. Brett was crying and I could hear Grandma and Stick Insect arguing. My father sounded very miserable.

* *Adrian's mother's boyfriend when she was separated from her husband*

I had a long talk with Mr Lambert after school. He took me to a café and bought me a cup of tea and a cake. He said, "Look, Adrian, try to separate yourself from the difficult situation your parents are in. You're a very intelligent boy and you mustn't let them pull you down to their level." 'A very intelligent boy!' At last someone apart from Pandora recognises my intellectual ability.

Had my biology exam. I was the last to finish.

Friday, September 17th.

Nearly everyone in our class has made an appointment with Mr Lambert to talk about their family problems. Even Pandora, whose mother is a marriage guidance counsellor!

Mr Lambert's looking worried. He's constantly biting his nails and has stopped taking people to the café.

Sunday, September 19th.

Went to see Bert and Queenie today. They were hostile to me because I haven't been to see them for a week. Bert said, "He doesn't care about old people any more. He just wants to enjoy himself." How unfair! I can't remember the last time I enjoyed myself. Queenie didn't say anything because she can't speak, but she certainly *looked* hostile. Bert ordered me to come back tomorrow to tidy up. Their cleaning lady comes on Tuesdays and Bert likes the house to be tidy for when she comes.

Monday, September 20th.

My mother's cheque from the Social Security didn't come. I'm very worried.

I was amazed to find out that I only got average marks for my exams. There must have been a serious mistake.

Friday, September 24th.

Still no cheque from the Social Security. But a cheque from my father arrived, so we're saved. My mother gave me 15p for a Mars bar, my first in 10 days.

My mother took the cheque to the bank this morning, but they told her it would take four days until she could **cash** it. However, the manager agreed to lend her £25.

Saturday, September 25th.

Looked up 'pregnancy' in the *Family Health Encyclopedia*. I was interested to see that 'Pregnancy' was next to 'Sex and Reproduction'. Started to read a section called 'Testes and Sperm' and was surprised to learn that my testes make several hundred million sperm *a day*. Where do they all go? I know that some escape during the night, but what about the rest?

Sunday, September 26th.

Read the whole of 'Sex and Reproduction' in bed last night. Woke up to find that a few hundred million sperm had escaped. It will give the remaining sperm some room to move about.

Wednesday, September 29th.

Still no cheque from the Social Security!

We studied semen in biology today. I was able to give a full description of the life cycle of a sperm. The biology teacher was very impressed. He said, "Mole, I don't know if you've got a natural talent for biology or if you're obsessed with sex. If it's the latter, perhaps you should talk to the school psychologist." I assured the teacher that my interest was purely scientific.

CHAPTER 6

October

Saturday, October 2nd.

Courtney Elliot brought a letter from my mother's parents. They're not exactly sympathetic to our problems. They seem more worried about a sock that was lost in our house when they were here at Christmas.

Sunday, October 3rd.

My mother wrote a sarcastic reply to her parents' letter. She also offered them her last pound note to buy a new pair of socks. I begged her not to send the letter. She said she would consider the matter and she put the letter behind the biscuit tin.

Tuesday, October 5th.

Still no cheque from the Social Security. My mother phoned the local radio station and told them she was going to abandon her child at the Social Security office unless she was given her cheque. Everybody who was listening to the radio heard her! We sat and waited for the phone to ring. At 12.30 my mother said, "Put on your coat, Adrian, I'm taking you to be abandoned." As we were leaving, the phone rang. It was my father. He asked us not to mention his name on the radio.

There were radio reporters and journalists at the Social Security offices. Everyone wanted to tell them their problems. There was so much disorder that the police had to come.

I was only abandoned for 45 minutes before my mother was given an emergency cheque. They said it would be enough money for the weekend.

Wednesday, October 6th.

There was a picture of my mother and me on the front page of the local paper tonight. The headline said A MOTHER'S TORMENT. In the article, it said that my mother was 58 and that I was five.

Thursday, October 7th.

One of the younger pupils asked me for my autograph at school today. She said, "I saw your photo in the paper today and told my mother that you go to my school, but she said that's impossible because you're only five. So I want your autograph to show that I know you."

My mother phoned the local paper and insisted that they print the following correction:

Mrs Mole is 38 and not 58, as was reported in Wednesday's edition.

My mother's fed up with the neighbours talking. Last night one of them called out, "You're a good-looking woman for your age, Mrs Mole."

Saturday, October 9th.

The Guinness Book of Records phoned today. They asked my mother if she would mind her name being included in the 'Oldest Women to

3 Making inferences helps you understand things that aren't actually written in the text. What can you infer from the sentences below? Choose the correct answer according to the story.

1. "Only one piece of bacon per plate."
   a. Bernard Porke wasn't a very generous man.
   b. Bernard Porke didn't like bacon.
2. "We sat on the beach and he told us he was the father of Stick Insect's one-day-old baby boy. About 60 hours passed."
   a. Adrian was distracted.
   b. Adrian felt uncomfortable when his father told him the news.
3. "At last someone apart from Pandora recognises my intellectual ability."
   a. Adrian is confident that he's intelligent.
   b. Pandora would be the last person to think that Adrian is intelligent.
4. "They seem more worried about a sock that was lost in our house when they were here at Christmas."
   a. Adrian's grandparents haven't got money to buy socks.
   b. Adrian's grandparents aren't very sympathetic to the Moles.

4 Answer the questions. Write the answers in your notebook.

1. How did Adrian expect his Grandma to react to the news of the illegitimate child? Was he correct?
2. How do you think Adrian felt about his new brother?
3. What did Adrian offer to do while the Braithwaites were on holiday and what was he really planning to do?
4. Why do you think Mr Lambert stopped taking pupils to the café?
5. What made Adrian change his mind about taking part in the school play?

CHAPTER 7

November

Monday, November 1st.

After school I went to the hairdresser's with my enormous mother. She didn't want me to go with her, but I can't let her go out on her own, can I? Women are always having babies in phone boxes, buses, lifts, etc.

My mother let the hairdresser cut her hair very short and spray it purple! Not only did she pay him for doing it, but she also gave him a **tip**!

My mother let the hairdresser cut her hair very short and spray it purple!

Thursday, November 4th.

My father phoned today and asked me how my mother was. I said she was as well as could be expected, for an eight-and-a-half-months-pregnant woman. I asked him how his own baby was. He said, "That's right, Adrian. Make me feel bad." Then he put the phone down.

Sunday, November 7th.

Went to see Bert and Queenie with my mother. Everyone we met on the way made comments like, "I expect you'll be glad when the baby's born." My mother's replies weren't very polite.

Bert opened the door. He said, "Haven't you had that horrible baby yet?" My mother said, "Shut up, you stupid geriatric." Why can't people be polite to each other? You would never guess that my mother and Bert like each other.

Everyone was too old, or too ill, or too pregnant to do any cooking, so we ate bread and cheese for our Sunday dinner. Then we took it in turns to teach Queenie to speak again. I got her to say 'a jar of beetroot, please' very clearly. I might be a speech therapist when I grow up.

Wednesday, November 10th.

My mother has gone mad; she's cleaning the whole house. She's taken all the curtains down. Now everybody passing by in the street can look in the window and see our most intimate moments. I was examining my spots in the living-room mirror when one of the neighbours shouted from the street, "There's a lovely big spot on the back of your neck." Only now do I understand the importance of curtains in civilised English life.

Thursday, November 11th.

When I got home from school, my mother was nowhere in the house, but I found a note on the table. It said:

I'm in the Royal Hospital. Call a taxi. £5 note at bottom of spaghetti jar. Don't worry.
Love, Mum

When I got to the hospital, my mother was lying on a high bed, reading. She was pleased to see me, but suddenly she seemed to be in pain and then began to sing. A nurse asked her if she was OK. My mother said, "Yes. This is Adrian." The nurse said, "Put on a mask and gown, Adrian, and sit in a corner. Things will start happening soon."

After about half an hour, my mother was singing more and talking less. She held my hand very tightly. The nurse came back and told me to go out, but my mother **wouldn't release** my hand. So the nurse told me to time the contractions.

At 5.19 p.m. the doctor said, "It's a lovely little girl, Mrs Mole." He looked very pleased, as if he were the father himself. The baby started crying and she was put on my mother's stomach. I congratulated my mother and she said, "Say hello to your sister."

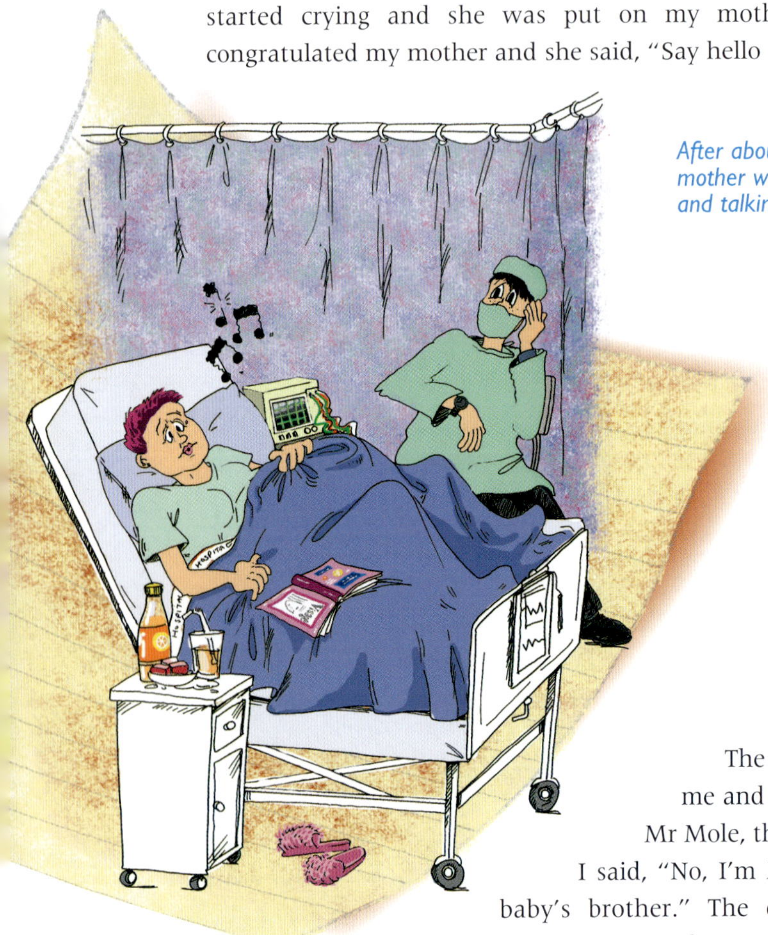

After about half an hour, my mother was singing more and talking less.

The doctor looked at me and said, "Aren't you Mr Mole, the baby's father?" I said, "No, I'm Master Mole, the baby's brother." The doctor was very angry and asked me to leave. So I went and sat in the waiting-room.

At 6.15 I phoned Pandora and told her the news. She shouted for joy. Next, I phoned Grandma, who cried. Then I phoned Bert and Queenie, who threatened to come and see my mother, but I persuaded them not to. Then I went home.

I tried to imagine sharing the house with a little girl. I put all my fragile possessions on the top shelf in my room. Then I went to bed. The phone woke me an hour later. It was my father. He wanted to know every detail about his daughter. I said that she looked like him. Half bald and angry-looking.

Friday, November 12th.

I'm a hero at school. Everyone thinks that *I* **delivered** the baby. The dinner lady gave me an extra big portion of chips. After school I went to the hospital to see my female relatives.

I'm staying at Pandora's house. At dinner I gave them a detailed description of the birth. Mr Braithwaite suddenly got up and left the table.

Saturday, November 13th.

Pandora and I went to see my mother and the baby this afternoon. There was a crowd of visitors round her bed. Then Bert and Queenie arrived and we had to make room for them. A nurse said, "You're only allowed two visitors to a bed." Just then Grandma and my father arrived, so everyone was pleased to go and leave them with my mother.

Sunday, November 14th.

My mother's coming home at 10.30 tomorrow morning. I asked if I should order a taxi but she said, "No, your father is driving us home." *Us*! I'm no longer an only child.

Monday, November 15th.

Didn't go to school today. At 11.15 I saw the strange sight of my father carrying his daughter into the house, followed by my purple-haired mother. I haven't got enough emotions to manage all the complications of my life. The atmosphere was rather tense, so I made some tea. My mother took her tea to bed. After a few minutes my father went back to Grandma's.

Wednesday, November 17th.

The baby woke up five times in the night. I know, because I sat beside her, checking her breathing every 10 minutes.

Pandora says I'm beginning to get boring about the baby. She says my sister's feeding habits aren't of any interest to her.

My father was ironing baby clothes when I got home from school. He said, "If you laugh, I'll kill you." My mother was feeding the baby, with her feet on the dog's back. It was a charming family picture, only ruined when my father went 'home' to his other family.

My father was ironing baby clothes when I got home from school.

Friday, November 19th.

I asked my mother what she was going to call the baby. She said she didn't know. I suggested we both make a list.

My mother's list: Charity, Christobel, Zoe, Jade, Frankie, India, Rosie, Caitlin, Ruth

My list: Tracy, Claire, Toyah, Diana, Pandora, Sharon

I only like 'Rosie' and 'Ruth' from my mother's list. She didn't like any on my list, not even Pandora. I think it's the most beautiful girl's name in the history of the world. Whenever I say it or hear it, I get a bursting feeling in my chest.

Saturday, November 20th.

My sister's name is Rosie Germaine Mole. Everybody likes Rosie, but only my mother likes Germaine. We registered her birth today. We went to the municipal offices and filled in a form giving her name, date of birth, etc. Then we celebrated by going to a café for a meal. Rosie was very good. She only woke up once when my mother dropped a warm chip on her head.

Tuesday, November 23rd.

Horrible Lucas phoned tonight. My mother spoke to him quietly for 10 minutes, as if she didn't want me to hear. But I heard the last thing she said before she threw the phone across the hall, because she shouted at the top of her voice, "ALL RIGHT – HAVE A BLOOD TEST!"

Perhaps Lucas thinks he's got a fatal blood disease. I hope he has.

Friday, November 26th.

I got a terrible shock when I came out of school today. Stick Insect was waiting for me, with Maxwell and Brett. Maxwell shouted, "Hello brother." I pushed a bit of Mars bar into his mouth before he could embarrass me more. I introduced Pandora to Stick Insect and then asked Stick Insect why she had waited for me. She told me that my father was terrible to live with, and that Grandma was worse. I said, "What can I do about it?" Stick Insect said, "I just wanted to tell somebody." Then she went back to Grandma's. Adults are all mad.

Changed my first nappy tonight. Tomorrow I'm going to try doing it with my eyes open.

Sunday, November 28th.

How can my mother change Rosie's horrible nappy and at the same time smile and even laugh? I nearly **fainted** when I tried to do it. Perhaps women's sense of smell is not as well-developed as men's.

Monday, November 29th.

My mother hasn't been paying any attention to me since Rosie was born. She was never a very attentive mother – I always had to clean my own shoes – but recently I feel emotionally **deprived**. I'm spending most of the time reading in my room.

Tuesday, November 30th.

Made my Christmas present list in order of preference.

Big present list: computer (no chance), colour TV, music centre, 3/4 length sheepskin coat (for warmth and status)

Small present list: pair of trousers, Adidas trainers, Adidas anorak, desk lamp, gold pen (with my name on it), electric razor

Things I always get whether I want them or not: coloured pens, false nose / glasses

I gave my mother the list, but she wasn't in the mood for talking about Christmas. In fact, just mentioning Christmas put her in a bad mood.

CHAPTER 8

December

Wednesday, December 1st.

We got an emotional phone call from Grandma. Stick Insect has taken Maxwell and Brett to stay with Maxwell's father, who has just come back from the Middle East with lots of money and toy camels. Apparently my father doesn't mind not living with his son, and Maxwell's father doesn't mind that Stick Insect had a baby. Stick Insect and Maxwell's father are getting married as soon as he gets his divorce.

Am I the only moral person left in our society?

Saturday, December 4th.

I'm having a **nervous breakdown**. Nobody has noticed yet. So I went to see Bert; he's my last hope. (Pandora said my mental state was caused by eating meat.) I told Bert I was having a nervous breakdown. He asked what was causing it. I said it was because there were no morals in our society. Bert said, "Idiot, what you need is a lot of hard work. You can start by washing the dishes."

Monday, December 6th.

I was woken up at 1 a.m., 2.30 a.m. and 4 a.m. by Rosie crying. At 8.30 a.m. I went into my mother's room to ask for my dinner money and found Rosie sleeping in my mother's bed. This is forbidden by the baby books. I checked that Rosie could breathe properly, took £3 out of my mother's purse, went to school and tried to behave normally.

Tuesday, December 7th.

Queenie died in her sleep at 3 o'clock this morning. Bert said it was a good way to go, and I agree with him. It was strange to go into Bert's house and see Queenie's things everywhere. I still can't believe that she's dead. I didn't let Bert see me crying and he didn't let me see him crying. But I know he's been crying. There are no clean handkerchiefs in his cupboard.

Pandora's father came to see us. He's going to make all the preparations for Queenie's funeral.

Saturday, December 11th.

Bert doesn't have enough money to pay for a nice funeral for Queenie. He's very unhappy. He said, "I wanted my girl to leave us properly!" I spent the whole evening phoning everyone who knew Queenie and getting them to donate money. I was called a saint several times.

Monday, December 13th.

It was Queenie's funeral today. When we got to Bert's house, he was sitting on the sofa wearing his wedding suit. My mother gave Bert a kiss. Bert said, "I don't like to think about her lying in a cold box. She never did like the cold."

We arrived at the crematorium. The funeral service was very short. We sang Queenie's favourite Christmas carol and her favourite song. Then, accompanied by sad music, Queenie slowly disappeared behind purple curtains. I watched in horror. Bert said, "Goodbye, old girl."

I was so shocked, I could hardly walk out of the room. Pandora and I both looked up when we got outside. Smoke was coming out of the chimney. Queenie always wanted to fly.

The funeral tea was in Pandora's house; it was very cheerful. Bert was OK and even told a few jokes. But he's on his own again and will need to be looked after more than ever!

How will I manage? I've got my exams in June.

Wednesday, December 15th.

We put up the Christmas tree at home tonight. It was a bit **rusty**, but I tied silver paper round the worst parts. The tree looked OK when we had finished. I picked Rosie up and showed her the finished tree, but she wasn't interested.

I bought a packet of cheap Christmas cards, but I haven't written on them yet. I'll wait and see who sends me one first.

Sunday, December 19th.

My father phoned to ask what we were doing at Christmas. My mother said, "The usual seasonal things, George: eating turkey, getting drunk, buying replacement lights for the Christmas tree." My father said, "Mother and I will be having a quiet time, on our own, alone. Just the two of us." My mother said, "It sounds wonderful. Well, I must go. A crowd of pre-Christmas guests have just arrived with the champagne."

This was a complete lie. It was only me coming into the room with a cup of tea.

Monday, December 20th.

School finishes tomorrow, so everyone is a little wild. The girls are doing no work at all. They just sit in the classrooms, count how many Christmas cards they've received from each other and write hundreds more. I haven't sent any cards at all yet. I'm still waiting to see if anybody sends me one.

Tuesday, December 21st. Last day of school

Thank God! I got seven Christmas cards. Three were in good taste. The other four were in very bad taste and printed on poor quality paper that won't stand up. I quickly wrote out seven cards and gave them to a pupil to deliver.

Wednesday, December 22nd.

Took £15 out of my bank account today. I know it's a lot of money, but I've got an extra person to buy for: Rosie.

9.30 p.m. I forgot that Queenie isn't here any more. I didn't need to spend so much money. My memory!

Thursday, December 23rd.

Made a gift list and then went to Woolworth's, as they've got a good selection of Christmas gifts.

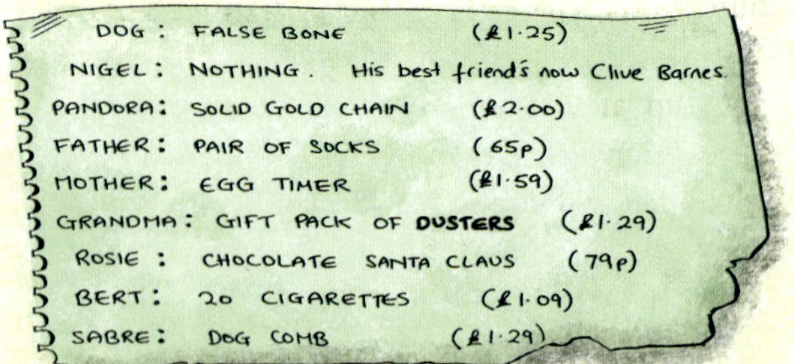

Made a gift list and then went to Woolworth's.

Woolworth's was so full of last-minute shoppers that I had to queue for half an hour to pay. Why do people wait to do their shopping until there are only two days left before Christmas?

Went to the Youth Club party with Pandora. Nigel caused a scandal by dancing with Clive Barnes, who was wearing lipstick and mascara! Everyone was saying that Nigel is gay – homosexual – so I made sure that everyone knew that he's no longer my best friend. At the end of the party they played *White Christmas* and all the couples danced romantically together. I told Pandora how much I adored her, and she said, "Aidy, my love, how long will our happiness last?" Pandora always ruins everything. Took her home. Kissed her twice. Went home. Fed dog. Checked Rosie's pulse. Went to bed.

Friday, December 24th. Christmas Eve

My mother's busy with Rosie, so I've had to do all the Christmas preparations. I got up at 7.30 and queued at the butcher's to buy a turkey. By 9 a.m. I was in the queue at the greengrocer's; at 2 p.m. I was at the grocer's with a long shopping list and Rosie's pram to carry everything home.

At 4 p.m. I was at Woolworth's to buy Christmas tree lights. I had to wait 10 minutes to be served and then there were none left. I tried every other shop I could think of. I got home at 6.15 after buying lights in a shop which is just round the corner from the house.

My mother had made the room look really nice, and when we'd finished decorating it, it looked like a room on a Christmas card. My mother and I had a quick drink before Bert arrived. We put him in front of the TV with a beetroot sandwich and went into the kitchen to start preparing the meal.

1 a.m. Just got back from midnight service. It was very emotional, though I think it was a mistake to have a real donkey in the church.

Saturday, December 25th. Christmas Day

Got up at 7.30. Had a wash and a shave, cleaned my teeth, squeezed my spots, then went downstairs and put the kettle on. My mother fed and cleaned Rosie, and I did the same to Bert. Then we opened our presents. I was very disappointed when I saw the shape of my present. I could see immediately that it didn't contain a single microchip. OK, a sheepskin coat is warm, but there's nothing you can *do* with it except wear it. But my mother was delighted with her egg timer. She said, "Wow, another one for my collection." Rosie ignored the chocolate Santa I bought her. That's 79p wasted!

I was glad when Aunt Susan and her friend, Gloria, arrived at 11 o'clock. Gloria's very glamorous and sexy. She wears very feminine clothes and has got a sexy voice. I don't know why she's friends with Aunt Susan, who's a prison officer, smokes cigars and has got hairy fingers. While my mother was cutting up the turkey, Bert looked at the top of Gloria's dress and said, "Give me a piece of breast." Gloria wasn't shocked at all, but I went very red and **pretended** to look for my serviette under the table.

While my mother was cutting up the turkey, Bert looked at the top of Gloria's dress.

I was given a glass of wine and talked brilliantly and amusingly for an hour, but then my mother told me to leave the table. "One drop of drink," she said, "and he can't keep his mouth shut."

In the evening I went to see Grandma and my father. Grandma forced me to eat some Christmas cake. My father didn't talk to me; he was completely drunk in an armchair.

Sunday, December 26th.

Pandora and I exchanged presents by candlelight in my bedroom. I put the solid gold chain round her neck and she put a 70% wool, 10% cashmere, 20% acrylic scarf round my neck. A cashmere scarf at 15!

Pandora was delighted with the solid gold chain. She kept looking at herself in the mirror. She said, "Thank you, darling, but how do you have enough money to buy solid gold? It must have cost you at least a hundred pounds!" I didn't tell her that it was a cheap chain from Woolworth's.

Monday, December 27th.

I've just received a note from Pandora, cancelling our planned trip to the cinema today. She woke up this morning with an ugly **rash** round her neck. It seems she is allergic to non-precious metal!

Tuesday, December 28th.

Walked up and down the High Street in my sheepskin coat and cashmere scarf. Saw Nigel in his new leather trousers. He told me he was trying to decide which kind of sexuality to choose: homo, bisexual or hetero. I asked him which he felt most comfortable with. He said, "All three, Moley." Nigel never could make decisions.

Friday, December 31st.

Bert has asked if he can stay till New Year's Day. My mother agreed, but she took me into the kitchen and whispered, "Bert can't live here forever, Adrian. I can't look after a small baby and a geriatric at the same time!"

At 11 o'clock my father phoned to wish us all a Happy New Year. My mother's face went a bit funny and she invited him round for a drink.

My mother looks really nice again now that her figure's nearly back to normal. My father arrived at one minute to 12. At midnight, we all stood round Bert's chair, kissed and wished each other Happy New Year.

Pandora phoned at 1 a.m. to say Happy New Year. The Braithwaites' party sounded good. I wish I'd gone there instead of being kind and staying at home. Went to bed terribly scared. I have my big exams this year.

CHAPTER 9

January

Saturday, January 1st, 1983. New Year's Day

These are my New Year's resolutions:

1) I will study at least two hours a night for my exams.
2) I will stop thinking erotic thoughts during school hours.
3) I will try to like Bert Baxter's dog.
4) I will get my mother and father together again.

Sunday, January 2nd.

I've only grown five or six centimetres since last year, so I suppose I must accept the fact that I will be one of those people who never get a good view in the cinema.

My skin is covered in spots, my ears stick out and my hair won't look fashionable no matter how I comb it.

Negotiations are taking place between my parents for a return to their married state. My mother said, "How can it work, Adrian? There's so much to forget." I suggested hypnosis.

Tuesday, January 4th.

More negotiations behind closed doors. As he left, I asked my father if it had been a good meeting. He said, "No comment!" and got in his car.

Wednesday, January 5th.

Negotiations have broken down. I heard a dish crashing to the kitchen floor, then a lot of shouting. Then the door slammed.

A message was passed to an intermediary (me) that new negotiations would be welcome. The message was passed on and the response was favourable, so I was asked to organise the time, place and baby-sitting details.

Friday, January 7th.

The meeting took place in a Chinese restaurant at 8 p.m. Negotiations continued all evening and only stopped when one party returned home to feed the baby.

Saturday, January 8th.

Both parties have made the following agreement:

It is agreed that Pauline Monica Mole and George Arthur Mole will try to live in mutual harmony for a trial period of one month. If the following agreement is broken during that time, divorce proceedings will automatically follow. The agreement:

1) G.A.M. will do his share of the housework, cheerfully, and without being told to.
2) P.M.M. will keep her side of the bedroom in a hygienic and presentable condition.
3) Both parties will go to the pub at Sunday lunchtimes.
4) The children of the marriage will be given equal attention by both parents.
5) Financial matters will be discussed each Friday night at 7 p.m.
6) A separate bank account will be opened for P.M.M.
7) Neither party will have a relationship with the opposite sex without the full knowledge and consent of the other party.
8) P.M.M. will not constantly mention the Doreen Slater episode. G.A.M. will not constantly mention the Lucas episode.

My sister and I were the witnesses. Rosie signed the agreement with an X.

Monday, January 10th.

Horrible school started today. My sheepskin made quite an impression everywhere it went – and it went everywhere. It's too valuable to leave in the cloakroom. Pandora and I held hands at assembly, but the headmaster saw us and shouted at us. I consoled Pandora in the boys' toilets in the break.

I consoled Pandora in the boys' toilets in the break.

I explained that the headmaster was probably impotent, and it made him angry to see young lovers in the prime of life.

Wednesday, January 12th.

Nigel has formed a Gay Club at school. He's the only member so far, but it will be interesting to see who else joins.

Thursday, January 13th.

The headmaster has ordered the closure of the Gay Club. He said that the school couldn't allow the gym to be used for immoral purposes. Nigel pretended to be innocent. He said, "But sir, the Gay Club is for pupils who want to enjoy themselves during the break. What is immoral about gaiety?" The headmaster said, "Nigel, the meaning of the word has changed over the years. It no longer just means 'cheerful', it now means something different." Nigel said, "What does it mean, sir?" The headmaster didn't answer, he obviously didn't want to say that 'gay' means 'homosexual'. So Nigel said, "Sorry, sir, I'll have to get an **up-to-date** dictionary!"

Sunday, January 16th.

I had to look after Rosie while my parents went to the pub. I pretended not to notice that her nappy needed to be changed, and acted surprised when my mother came back and said there was a terrible smell in the room.

Now I come to a difficult entry. How do I feel about my father's return home? He's been home for a week now and I've had lots of time to think about it, but they've had these reconciliations before and they've ended in tragedy. So I think I'll wait until the kissing has stopped and they're back to normal.

Saturday, January 22nd.

Went into town with Pandora, who wanted to buy a pair of neon-pink tights. We went into 50 shops, but none of the shops had neon pink, so Pandora's going to London to buy some. She said, "I really hate the provinces!"

Sunday, January 23rd.

Horrible Lucas phoned today. I told him that my mother was at the pub with my father. He asked me which pub, so I told him, and then he asked me lots of questions about Rosie. Then he said a strange thing; he said, "That's my girl!"

My parents came home in a very bad mood. It seems that my mother left the pub's darts match at a very important point to answer a telephone call.

Tuesday, January 25th.

Amazing! Super! Brilliant! The water workers have **gone on strike**, so we can't have showers at school! The twice-weekly torture of everyone seeing my inferior muscles is finished! I hope the water workers continue the strike until I've left full-time education.

Saturday, January 29th.

Bert Baxter phoned to ask why I hadn't been to see him. I said I'd been too busy, but I promised to go round tomorrow after dinner. Bert said, "Dinner? What's that?" I said, "You remember, Bert, it's meat, potatoes and vegetables." I invited him for dinner tomorrow, but when I told my parents, they were furious. They said they wanted to go and look at new houses tomorrow and were planning to get a Chinese take-away.

New houses? Why didn't they consult me? I've got my exams this year and it's very important that I don't have any drastic changes in my life.

CHAPTERS 7-9 ACTIVITIES

1 The sentences below are illogical. Make them logical by making any necessary changes. Do not change the words in bold.

1. He's **drunk** so he shouldn't eat now.

   ....

2. It was such a strange **sight**. I'll never forget leaving it.

   ....

3. I want to **exchange** this sweater. It looks great on me.

   ....

4. I had to **queue** for half an hour to sleep.

   ....

5. She **manages** her appearance and her job.

   ....

6. She was rude because she wanted to **make an impression**.

   ....

2 Match each word to the correct definition.

1. forbidden
2. witness
3. crowd
4. purpose
5. delighted
6. cheerful
7. pay attention

.... a. a large group of people
.... b. prohibited
.... c. very happy about something
.... d. a person who sees an event, crime or accident
.... e. in a good mood
.... f. the reason something is done or exists
.... g. notice or concentrate on something

3 Complete the sentences.

1. The doctor at the hospital thought Adrian was ....
2. When Adrian talks about his sister, Pandora ....
3. When Queenie died, Bert couldn't ....
4. Adrian made sure that everyone knew he was no longer Nigel's best friend because ....
5. Adrian didn't tell Pandora that the necklace ....
6. Adrian was happy that the water workers were on strike because ....

4 Answer the questions. Write the answers in your notebooks.

1. Why was Adrian upset the day his mother came home from hospital?
2. In what ways has Adrian taken on the role of a father to his baby sister?
3. Why did Adrian spend a lot of time reading in his room?
4. Why was Adrian asked to leave the Christmas dinner table?
5. Why did Pandora cancel the trip to the cinema?
6. What does Lucas suspect?

Did you know?

Around the world, people exchange Christmas greeting cards as part of the traditional celebration of Christmas. In 2004, the German post office gave away 20 million scented stickers to make Christmas cards smell like a Christmas tree, cinnamon, gingerbread or a baked apple.

CHAPTER 10

February

Wednesday, February 2nd.

Lucas arrived at our house this evening demanding to see Rosie. My father said that Rosie was busy and couldn't be disturbed, but Lucas started shouting, so my father let him in to stop the neighbours talking.

Lucas said, "Pauline, I want to see my child!" and my mother went very pale. My father sat down on the sofa and said weakly, "Pauline, tell me that Rosie is mine!"

"Of course she's yours, George!" my mother replied. Lucas took out his diary and said that he and my mother had slept together on March 13th when she went to a protest march in Sheffield. My father shouted, "Adulteress!"

"I'm not an adulteress," my mother said and started to cry. Lucas tried to put his arms round her, but she gave him a karate chop on the back of his neck. Everybody had forgotten I was there until I ran from the room, saying, "I can't stand this eternal insecurity!"

On the way to my room, I passed Rosie in her cot. She was playing with her feet. She didn't know that they were discussing who her father was downstairs.

Thursday, February 3rd.

It seems that during the month of March last year both my parents were having secret relationships, which resulted in the birth of two children. But my diary for that period only has entries about my childish 14-year-old problems.

Pandora is giving me all her help at this time of crisis. She is a true friend.

Friday, February 4th.

I had to spend the day in the school doctor's room as I felt weak in the first lesson. The doctor asked me if there was anything wrong at home. I started to cry. "Adults have got complicated lives, Adrian," the doctor explained. I said that parents ought to be moral and have principles. "That's a lot to ask," the doctor replied.

I made her promise not to tell anyone that she'd seen me crying. She let me stay until my eyes were normal again.

Saturday, February 5th.

Lucas continues to torment us. A lawyer's letter arrived today. He's going to **take us to court** unless he's allowed to see Rosie.

Decided to go and see Grandma. I didn't tell her about Lucas. Another shock could kill her. She said that after the Stick Insect scandal, her hair fell out and hasn't grown back. This explains why she was wearing her hat in the house.

Tuesday, February 8th.

My father won't talk to Pandora's mother, who's a marriage guidance counsellor. Rosie's getting a tooth. Saliva comes out of her mouth all the time. She looks like a mad dog.

I don't know how I'm surviving the long school day. I'm walking around like a smiling robot, but inside I'm very sad.

The trial period for my mother and father finishes today. The two parties have agreed to an extension.

Saturday, February 12th.

The atmosphere at home is terrible, so I went to see Bert. I cleaned the house and took Sabre for a walk round the park. Barry Kent and his **gang** were there, but with Sabre by my side I didn't feel afraid.

Sunday, February 13th.

It's Valentine's Day tomorrow. I don't think I'll go to school. I hate being the only kid who doesn't come into the classroom with lots of cards. I know I'll get one from Pandora, but that's not the same; I've been going out with her for more than a year.

Monday, February 14th. St. Valentine's Day

Got four cards: one from Pandora, one from Grandma, one from my mother and one from Rosie. Wonderful!

I got Pandora a Cupid card and a mini box of chocolates. Lucas sent Rosie a card. My parents didn't bother this year – they're saving their money.

Tuesday, February 15th.

Pandora isn't speaking to me because I stupidly wrote 'Best Wishes' in her Valentine's card. She said it was a sign of our deteriorating relationship. I think she could be right. I don't like her so much any more. She's too clever for me.

Thursday, February 17th.

I wrote a poem on the toilet wall at school today. The poem was about the future, or rather, the fact that there isn't one. I thought it was a good way of making my stupid classmates more politically **aware**.

Friday, February 18th.

I was sent to the headmaster today. He was told about my toilet poem. I asked him how he knew I'd written it. He said, "You signed it, idiot boy." I've been **suspended** for a week.

Sunday, February 20th.

Barry Kent and his gang came to my house today. Kent said, "We're going to town, you can come if you want." I was feeling lonely and depressed, so I went.

Hung around the deserted shopping centre with Barry and the gang. At the moment I enjoy being with criminal types.

Barry kindly gave me permission to call him 'Baz'.

Monday, February 21st.

Baz took me home and introduced me to his family. Mrs Kent asked, "Aren't you the boy who's had all the scandal?" "Yeah," I replied. "That's me, but so what?" Mr Kent told me to be more polite to his wife. I immediately apologised and remembered my manners. I got up and offered Mrs Kent the only chair in the room that wasn't broken.

I had a nice meal with the family – chip sandwiches with tomato sauce. When I'd got used to the strange smell in the house, I was able to relax for the first time in weeks.

She's too clever for me

Tuesday, February 22nd.

I got a note from Pandora. She wrote:

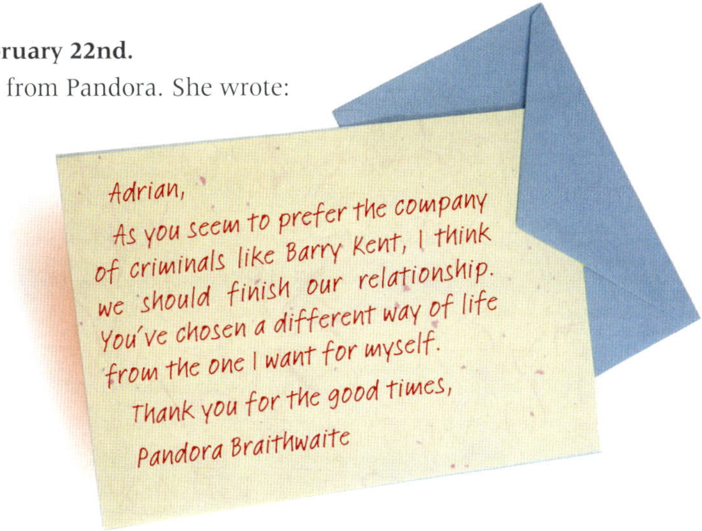
Adrian,

As you seem to prefer the company of criminals like Barry Kent, I think we should finish our relationship. You've chosen a different way of life from the one I want for myself.

Thank you for the good times,

Pandora Braithwaite

Spent the early part of the evening standing outside the pub with the gang. I made amusing observations about girls walking past and made the gang laugh. They call me 'Brains'.

Friday, February 25th.

Mrs Kent has decided to have some new furniture, so the gang and I went to the **rubbish tip** to see what we could find. We came back with two almost unbroken kitchen chairs, a basket for the dirty clothes and a rug. We're going back tomorrow with Rosie's pram to get a washing machine.

Saturday, February 26th.

I borrowed the pram, but unfortunately Rosie was in it. We had to take her out and carry her while we pushed the pram with the washing machine in it. But she didn't cry.

Mrs Kent was delighted with her new washing machine. Mr Kent took out the old motor and started cleaning it on the rug. Mrs Kent didn't say a word! My mother would have been furious.

Monday, February 28th.

Rosie's got her first tooth. My finger is still bleeding.

Spent the evening outside the Chinese chip shop throwing chips about with the gang. I haven't read a book for ages. Instead of reading about life, I'm living it.

CHAPTER 11

March

Thursday, March 3rd.

The community policeman, PC Gordon, has been to warn my parents that I'm running wild with a **notorious** gang. He's coming tomorrow to talk to me about being a responsible citizen.

Friday, March 4th.

PC Gordon is the type of person everybody likes. He said things like, "You're obviously a clever boy, Adrian" and "Kent and his gang are losers." Later my parents came in and said the usual things like, "He's a good boy at home" (my father) and "Barry Kent has influenced him" (my mother).

Saturday, March 5th.

Grandma phoned and said that everyone in the neighbourhood knew that I was "keeping bad company". She made me go round for tea. I didn't want to go, but Grandma has the kind of voice that makes you obey orders. She told me that my father had been in trouble with the police in 1953. She said, "He was caught stealing apples. The shock nearly killed me and your poor dead grandad." I wanted to know how they had persuaded my father to give up his life of crime. She said, "Your grandad hit him with his belt." Poor Dad! It explains why he's got so much anger inside him.

Sunday, March 6th.

Being in a gang isn't as exciting as I thought it would be. All we do is hang around shopping centres. Sometimes I wish I were in my bedroom, reading, with the dog at my side.

Sometimes I wish I were in my bedroom, reading, with the dog at my side

Tuesday, March 8th.

Arrived home after a cold, boring night of shouting in quiet streets. Barry Kent **knocked over** a rubbish bin for a laugh, but in fact it wasn't very funny, and I had to force myself to laugh with the others in the gang. After Barry had gone home, I collected the broken glass and put it back in the bin. I wouldn't like a little kid to fall on it.

I can't continue living this double life for much longer.

Friday, March 11th.

Pandora Braithwaite is going out with Brainbox Henderson. I hope they'll both be very happy. Nigel says they spend all their time talking about mathematics.

I've decided not to take my exams. I'm sure I'll fail them, so why waste all that time worrying?

Sunday, March 13th. Mothering Sunday

Horrible Lucas sent my mother a Mother's Day card signed 'Rosie'. Grandma sent Stick Insect a card signed 'Brett'. My mother sent Grandma Mole a card signed 'George'. My father sent my other grandma a card signed 'Pauline'. I didn't send my mother a card this year.

The police have arrested Barry Kent for taking flowers from the park. He said they were a present for his mother.

Barry Kent knocked over a rubbish bin for a laugh

Monday, March 14th.

Reasons for not living: you die anyway; life is full of torment; there is too much cruelty in the world; exams in June; my parents hate me; I've lost Pandora; nobody leaves Barry Kent's gang alive.

Reasons for living: things might get better.

Wednesday, March 16th.

Elizabeth Broadway keeps pulling my school scarf from my neck and running away with it, forcing me to chase her. This is a definite sign that she is romantically interested in me. I can feel my hormones moving for the first time in months.

Thursday, March 17th.

Elizabeth took my bag during break and ran away with it. I caught up with her in the bushes at the end of the sports field, and we spent a very enjoyable five minutes there. The climax was me taking off her glasses and hair pins. She looked different without her glasses and with long hair. I don't know what would have happened if the bell hadn't rung for the next lesson.

Friday, March 18th.

At last! My parents have noticed that I'm out of control and aren't allowing me to go out after school. Spent the evening reading.

I've written a letter to Barry Kent, **resigning** from the gang.

Monday, March 21st.

My parents have hardly spoken to me since Friday night. They're too busy watching Rosie's development.

Tuesday, March 22nd.

I've decided to leave home. Nobody will care. In fact my parents probably won't notice that I've gone.

Wednesday, March 23rd.

I'm making my preparations to leave. I've already written goodbye letters to Pandora, my parents, Bert, Grandma, Elizabeth, Baz, Nigel and a rather offensive letter to the headmaster.

Thursday, March 24th.

Five days to go. I'm growing a beard.

I've borrowed my dead grandad's suitcase. Luckily he had the same initials as me. His name was Arnold. Grandma thinks I'm using it for a camping trip with the Youth Club. The truth would kill her.

Friday, March 25th.

I've started packing my suitcase. I've made a list of all the essential clothes and equipment I'll have to take with me.

I'll have to **lower my standards** and only change my socks and underwear every two days.

No sign of the beard yet.

Sunday, March 27th.

My parents spent three hours forcing Rosie to sit up on her own, but she kept falling down and laughing. I told my parents that her back muscles weren't strong enough yet, but they wouldn't listen. They said, "She's much more advanced than you were at the age of four months!"

They'll regret these cruel words on Tuesday.

Tuesday, March 29th.

I spent the day packing and repacking. I couldn't decide what to take and what to leave behind. At 8.25 a.m. I left the house with the dog, took £50 out of my bank account and started walking northwards.

Wednesday, March 30th.

3 p.m. Watford Gap Service Station. I'm now on the M1 Motorway to the north of London. My first mistake was waiting **for a lift** on the southern side of the motorway. My second mistake was bringing the dog.

7.30 p.m. Sheffield. Got a lift in a lorry full of pigs. Just my luck! I'll have to be careful. Horrible Lucas lives in Sheffield. Why doesn't my beard grow?

9.30 p.m. Leeds. Listened to the 9 o'clock news but they said nothing about my mysterious disappearance. A man has just asked me if I want to sell the dog. I was tempted but I said no.

11 p.m. Phoned home but they didn't answer the phone immediately like they do in the films about **runaway** children. Another sign of their indifference.

Got a lift in a lorry full of pigs.

CHAPTER 12

April – June

Friday, April 1st. Good Friday

Thank God for launderettes! If they hadn't been invented, I'd be dead of hydrophobia by now. Nowhere else is open. It cost a *pound* to dry my sleeping bag, but I was so wet and cold that I didn't care at the time.

I'm 16 tomorrow, but there's still no sign of a beard.

Saturday, April 2nd.

Manchester Railway Station. Got here by fish lorry. Pretended to be asleep to avoid the driver's conversation.

10.30 a.m. I wonder what my mum and dad have bought me for my birthday. I hope they're not too worried. Perhaps I should phone them and tell them that I'm well and happy.

3 p.m. Nobody has said 'Happy Birthday' to me. I'm not well and I'm not happy. In fact, I'm extremely unhappy.

5.30 p.m. Bought myself a birthday card. Inside I wrote:

To our darling first-born child on his 16th birthday. With all the love it is possible to give.

From your admiring and loving parents

6.15 p.m. There was nothing about me on the news.

9.30 p.m. I've just phoned the police station, using a disguised voice. I said, "Adrian Mole, a 16-year-old runaway, is outside the Blood Transfusion Headquarters." Then I gave the policeman my description. He said, "April Fool's Day was yesterday."

10 p.m. Waited outside the Blood Transfusion place but there wasn't a policeman in sight. There's never a policeman when you need one.

11.39 p.m. I've walked past the police station 24 times, but no one's paid any attention to me.

Sunday, April 3rd. Easter Sunday. Manchester (the doorway of St Ignatius Church)

1 a.m. It's traditional for **the homeless** to sleep in church doorways, so why aren't the doorways more comfortable? They could give a blanket, couldn't they?

7.30 a.m. Got up at six. Had a wash in a bird bath. Found a shop and bought two chocolate Easter eggs. Ate one myself and gave the other to the dog. The poor thing was so hungry that it ate the paper as well. I hope it won't be ill. I haven't got enough money to pay for a vet. I've only got £15 left of the £50 I took with me.

Monday, April 4th.

9 a.m. I'm in the vicar's wife's bed. She found me in the doorway and took me to her home. She's a true Christian.

10 a.m. The vicar's wife has phoned my parents and asked them to come and get me. I asked her for my parents' reactions. She thought for a moment and said, "**Angry relief**, dear!" I haven't seen the vicar yet. He's still sleeping. I hope he doesn't mind that a stranger is in his wife's bed.

12.30 p.m. The vicar's just gone out. Thank God! What a bore! No wonder his poor wife sleeps in a separate bed.

6 p.m. My parents are making a great effort to get here. I wish they would hurry up. I can't stand the vicar's boring conversation any longer.

Tuesday, April 5th. Home. Bedroom

Well, there were no crowds of people in the street waiting to welcome me. Just my mother's pale, worried face at the window and my grandmother's even paler face behind her. My father doesn't talk when he's driving, so we hardly spoke all the way home, but my mother and Grandma said a great many things. Finally, I begged them to stop and went to bed.

Wednesday, April 6th.

Dr Grey has just left. He says that I'm suffering from a depressive illness caused by worry. I've got to rest in bed and there mustn't be any arguments in the family. My parents are full of **guilt**. I can't stop worrying about the offensive letter I sent to the headmaster before I left home.

Sunday, April 10th.

Lay in bed all day. Rosie was brought in to cheer me up, but her 'talking' irritated me so she was taken away. Bert Baxter was carried upstairs to visit me, but his 'Get out of bed, you lazy good-for-nothing' had no effect on me.

I've got to rest in bed and there mustn't be any arguments in the family.

Thursday, April 14th.

A sign that my parents are now sick with worry – they allowed Barry Kent into the house. But the news of the gang's activities had no effect, so he was taken out of the room.

Dr Grey has said that he doesn't know how to treat me. My parents have asked for a psychologist to come and see me.

Friday, April 15th.

Dr Donaldson, the psychologist, has just left my bedside after listening very seriously to my worries. He advised me about my worries one by one.

1) If you fail your exams, you can take them again next year, or never take them – like the Queen.
2) Of course your parents love you. They didn't sleep the whole time you were away.
3) You're not ugly. You're a pleasant, average-looking boy.
4) Your sister's paternity problems are nothing to do with you and there is nothing you can do to help.
5) I'll write to the headmaster and inform him that you were under great stress when you wrote the letter.
6) Pandora is in the category of insoluble problems.

Saturday, April 16th.

Grandma came to my room at 8 a.m. and ordered me out of bed! She said, "This has been going on for too long! Now get up and go and shave!" I replied that I needed more time to find myself. Grandma said, "And I need to wash your sheets!"

I spent the day sitting on the sofa.

Sunday, April 17th. Sofa

My parents are forcing themselves to sound cheerful when they speak to me. They're trying to bring me back to normal life by making me watch the news on TV. It was full of stories about murders, bombings and air disasters.

The school holidays start tomorrow. It's just my luck to be too ill to be able to enjoy the break.

Thursday, April 21st.

Pandora came to see me for 10 minutes. Brainbox Henderson stood outside, playing with his calculator. Perhaps he was trying to calculate how much he loves Pandora. Well, it won't be as much as me! Pandora's coming back tomorrow.

Friday, April 22nd.

Pandora came round at 5 p.m. Half an hour later we were in each other's arms.

Pandora went to Brainbox Henderson's house to tell him the news, but he was out buying diskettes, so she left a message on his computer. Getting Pandora back from him is a triumph of Art over Technology.

Monday, April 25th.

Went to visit Bert with Pandora and Rosie. He was very pleased to see us as he didn't have any cigarettes in the house. He smelt terrible, so Pandora and I put him in the bath. (Bert asked Pandora to cover her eyes.) Then I gave him a good wash while Pandora took Rosie and Sabre to get cigarettes.

When Pandora came back, we lifted Bert out of the bath. (Pandora promised to keep her eyes shut.) Then I dried him and put him into clean pyjamas. He looked lovely. Bert really needs to be looked after 24 hours a day by people who love him. The problem is that very few people can tolerate Bert for more than two or three days.

Friday, April 29th.

My father took Rosie and me to the bank to help him persuade the bank manager to lend him some money, but after hearing that both my parents were out of work, the manager said no. He said, "I'm saving you from yourself, Mr Mole. You'll thank me one day."

"No I won't. I'm taking my account to another bank," my father replied.

Saturday, April 30th.

My mother has decided that sugar is the cause of all the evil in the world and won't have it in the house. She smoked two cigarettes while she informed me of her decision.

Sunday, May 1st.

Today I heard my father say, "Well, it's the North Sea for me, Pauline." I ran into the kitchen and said, "Don't do it, Dad. The economy is going to improve!" My father looked puzzled. Perhaps he was surprised to hear such emotional words from me. I was surprised myself.

Tuesday, May 3rd. Back to school

Quite a few changes have taken place since I was last at school. Mr Lambert has got married and the headmaster is ill. He's had a nervous breakdown, so the deputy headmaster has taken his place. The school's a bit more relaxed now.

We spent the first day back being taught how to study for the exams.

6 p.m. Started studying English, biology and geography.

7 p.m. Decided to concentrate on one subject at a time. Chose English.

8 p.m. Finished studying when Bert Baxter phoned and asked for my help. His toilet is **blocked** again.

Thursday, May 5th.

My father has gone for an interview for a job on an **oil rig** in the North Sea. *My father working on an oil rig*! It's nearly as good as having a cowboy for a father! I hope he gets the job. He'll be away from home for two weeks in every month.

Saturday, May 7th.

Spent all day studying with Pandora in her mother's study. Our house is intolerable because my father's so angry that he didn't get the job on the oil rig. I told him not to buy the check shirts and jeans until he was sure he had the job, but he wouldn't listen. Now he owes Grandma £38.39. He borrowed the money from her to buy the clothes.

Monday, May 9th.

The Prime Minister has announced that there will be a general election on June 9th. How selfish can you be? Don't they know that May and early June are supposed to be a quiet time, while teenagers study for their exams?

I get an anxiety attack every time I think about the exams. I know I'm going to fail. My problem is that I'm *too* intellectual. I'm constantly thinking about things, like: was God married? My brain's so full of these thoughts that I forget *facts*.

Wednesday, May 11th.

Grandma has given me some brain pills to help me study for my exams. They're made from a horrible part of a bull. She said, "Your dead grandad thought they were wonderful." I took two this morning, but by the afternoon I still couldn't remember the capital of British Honduras.

Monday, May 16th.

My studying is being constantly interrupted by election candidates knocking at our front door and asking us to vote for them. Does nobody care about education in this country?

Wednesday, May 18th.

Another candidate (green suit, orange shirt, nervous smile) has just left our house almost in tears, because my mother wouldn't let her kiss Rosie.

Thursday, May 19th.

This morning I was shown a picture of a cottage in terrible condition, and asked if I would like to live there. I replied in the negative. My mother said, "It sounds perfect. It's three kilometres from the nearest shop, right in the country. Wouldn't you like to get up in the morning and feed the chickens, Adrian?"

I replied, "I hate chickens. They have cruel eyes."

Friday, May 20th.

The headmaster has retired because of ill health (he's gone mad), and the deputy headmaster has his name on the headmaster's door. I've never been taught by him, but everyone says he's a nice man, who talks about his family and who informs his class when he's thinking of buying a new car.

Saturday, May 21st.

My father told three politicians to get out of our garden this morning. He said, "My son's upstairs studying for a better future, and your demands for attention are disturbing him!"

Actually I was measuring my thing at the time, but their noise was disturbing me and I couldn't concentrate.

Saturday, May 28th.

Stayed in bed all day studying for my exams. Bert Baxter phoned three times, but each time I told my parents to tell him that I was out of town. The third time he phoned, my mother asked, "Was it anything important, Bert?" Bert said, "Not really. I just wanted to tell him that I think I'm 90 today."

I felt so bad that I pretended to return from out of town and went to see him. My visit seemed to do him good.

Tuesday, May 31st.

This will be my last entry until the exams are over.

Courtney Elliot is coming to help me study for my exams. Must stop, his taxi has just arrived.

Thursday, June 2nd.

My parents went to the pub last night. During their absence Pandora and I did some extremely heavy kissing and caressing; so heavy that I felt a weight fall from me.

If I don't pass my exams, it won't matter. I have known what it is to have the love of a good woman.

CHAPTERS 10-12 ACTIVITIES

1 Complete each sentence with a suitable word to show that you have understood the words in bold.

1. I want to **apologise**. I'm .... that I said those things to you.
2. Her behaviour is **childish**. She's not very ....
3. His appearance was **disguised** so he was hard to ....
4. What a **clever** little boy. His parents must be very ....
5. I'm feeling **relaxed** after my holiday. I'm no longer ....
6. He was **lonely** during the Christmas holiday. All his friends were ....

2 Complete each sentence with the correct word or phrase below.

1. Don't .... There's still a chance you can win.
2. He hasn't got any .... He's very rude.
3. Don't lie to me. I want to hear the ....
4. If you don't .... the law, you'll get into trouble.
5. We saw the policeman .... the thief for stealing.
6. He knows how to .... his friends well.

1. give up / hurry up
2. losers / manners
3. truth / chase
4. warn / obey
5. demand / arrest
6. treat / owe

3 Who did it? Match the characters to the correct continuation.

1. Mr and Mrs Mole
2. Grandma
3. The vicar's wife
4. Bert
5. The doctor
6. PC Gordon

.... a. asked Adrian if there was anything wrong at home.
.... b. warned Mr and Mrs Mole that Adrian was in a gang.
.... c. noticed that Adrian was out of control.
.... d. helped Adrian when he ran away from home.
.... e. convinced Adrian to get out of bed.
.... f. phoned Adrian three times because it was his birthday.

4 Answer the questions. Write the answers in your notebooks.

1. Why did Lucas think that Rosie was his child?
2. Why was Adrian suspended from school?
3. Why do you think Adrian joined Barry Kent's gang?
4. How and why did Adrian and Pandora finish their relationship?
5. Why did Adrian run away from home?
6. How did Adrian feel on his 16th birthday?
7. How long was Adrian in bed and why did he finally get up?

Did you know?

Fish and chips became a popular meal with the working class in Great Britain. This was a consequence of the rapid development of fishing in the North Sea and development of railways that connected ports to cities. In 1860, the first fish and chip shop was opened in London.

GLOSSARY

English	Castellano	Català
angry relief	enfado y alivio	enuig i alleujament
aware	conscientes	conscients
beetroot	(de) remolacha	(de) remolatxa
belly dancer	bailarina de la danza del vientre	ballarina de la dansa del ventre
bend down	agacharse	ajupir-se
blind date	cita a ciegas	cita a cegues
blocked	atascado	embussat
breasts	pechos; pechuga	pit(s)
broke down	se averió; fracasado	es va avariar; fracassat
bump	barriga, tripa	panxa
called me names	me insultaba	m'insultava
cash	cobrar en efectivo	cobrar en efectiu
cool	"guai" (col.)	"guai" (col·loq.)
delivered	asistí en el parto de	vaig assistir al part de
deprived	necesitado	necessitat
drowned	ahogara	ofegués
dusters	trapos del polvo	draps de la pols
embarrassed	avergonzado	avergonyit
fainted	me desmayé	em vaig desmaiar
fine	multa	multa
for a lift	que alguien me llevara / recogiera	que algú em portés / em recollís
gang	pandilla	colla
getting on well	llevando bien	portant bé
gone on strike	puesto en huelga	declarat en vaga
guilt	culpabilidad	culpabilitat
heating	calefacción	calefacció

GLOSSARY

English	Euskara	Galego
angry relief	haserrea eta lasaitua	anoxo e conforto
aware	ernea, ohartua	conscientes
beetroot	erremolatxa(zko)	(de) remolacha
belly dancer	sabel-dantzari	bailarina da danza do ventre
bend down	makurtu	anicarse
blind date	itsukako hitzordu	cita ás cegas
blocked	trabatua, butxatua	atoado
breasts	bularrak, bularki	peitos; peituga
broke down	matxuratu egin zen; porrot egindako	avariouse; fracasado
bump	gilbor	bandullo, tripa
called me names	iraintzen ninduen	insultábame
cash	dirutan kobratu	cobrar en efectivo
cool	primerako	"guai" (col.)
delivered	erditzen lagundu nion	asistín no parto de
deprived	gabetua	necesitado
drowned	itoko balitz	afogase
dusters	hauts-trapuak, zatarrak	panos do lixo
embarrassed	lotsarazi	avergoñara
fainted	zorabiatu nintzen	desmaieime
fine	isun	multa
for a lift	inork jasotzeko / eramateko	que alguén me levase / recollese
gang	lagun-talde	panda
getting on well	ongi moldatzen	levando ben
gone on strike	greban jarri	puxéronse en folga
guilt	erru	culpabilidade
heating	berokuntza	calefacción

GLOSSARY

English	Castellano	Català
hung around	di vueltas por	vaig donar voltes per
knocked over	volcó	va bolcar
longingly	con deseo	amb desig
lower my standards	bajar mi nivel	baixar el meu nivell
measure	medir	mesurar
nappy	pañal	bolquer
nervous breakdown	ataque de nervios	atac de nervis
notorious	muy conocida	molt coneguda
oil rig	plataforma petrolífera	plataforma marina de perforació
pity	compadezco a	compadeixo
pram	cochecito	cotxet
pretended	fingí	vaig fingir
prick	pinchar	punxar
punished	castigada	castigada
put my name down	inscrito, apuntado	inscrit, apuntat
rash	sarpullido	erupció, granissada
razor	maquinilla de afeitar	màquina d'afaitar
regretting	arrepintiéndose de	penedint-se de
rehearsals	ensayos	assaigs
resigning	dimitiendo	dimitint
roller-skating rink	pista de patinaje sobre ruedas	pista de patinatge sobre rodes

English	Euskara	Galego
hung around	itzulinguruka ibili nintzen	dei voltas por
knocked over	irauli zuen	verteu
longingly	irrikaz	con desexo
lower my standards	neure maila beheratu	baixar o meu nivel
measure	neurtu	medir
nappy	haur-oihal	cueiro
nervous breakdown	nerbioetako atake, urdurialdi	ataque de nervios
notorious	entzutetsu	moi coñecida
oil rig	petrolio-plataforma	plataforma petrolífera
pity	erruki dut	compadezo a
pram	haur-kotxe	cocheciño
pretended	itxura egin nuen, plantak egin nituen	finxín
prick	ziztatu	picar
punished	zigortua	castigada
put my name down	izena eman dut	inscrito, apuntado
rash	negal, legen	sarabullo
razor	bizarra mozteko	coitela de barbear
regretting	damuturik	arrepentíndose de
rehearsals	saioak, entseguak	ensaios
resigning	dimitituz	dimitindo
roller-skating rink	gurpil gainean patinatzeko pista	pista de patinaxe sobre rodas

GLOSSARY

English	Castellano	Català
rubbish tip	vertedero de basuras	abocador d'escombraries
runaway	escapados	que s'han escapat
rusty	oxidado	rovellat
sew	coser	cosir
slammed the door	dio un portazo	va donar un cop de porta
slipped	resbaló	va relliscar
so far	hasta ahora	fins ara
stick insect	insecto palo	insecte pal
string vest	camiseta de malla	samarreta de malla
stroke	derrame cerebral	vessament cerebral
support	apoyo	suport
suspended	expulsado	expulsat
swollen	hinchada	inflat
sympathetic	comprensiva	comprensiva
take us to court	demandarnos	demandar-nos
tax department	oficina / departamento de impuestos	oficina / departament d'impostos
the homeless	los sin techo	els sense sostre
threatened to report	amenazó con denunciar	va amenaçar en denunciar
tip	propina	propina
tore it up	lo rompió / hizo pedazos	va trencar / esmicolar
up-to-date	actualizado	actualitzat
wouldn't release	no me soltaba	no deixava anar
yashmak	velo (que llevan algunas musulmanas)	vel (que porten algunes musulmanes)

GLOSSARY

English	Euskara	Galego
rubbish tip	zabortegi	vertedoiro do lixo
runaway	iheslariak	fuxidos
rusty	herdoildua	oxidado
sew	josi	coser
slammed the door	atea danbateko batez itxi zuen	deu un golpe coa porta
slipped	irrist egin zuen	esvarou
so far	orain arte	até agora
stick insect	intsektu-makila	insecto pau
string vest	mailazko elastiko	camisola de malla
stroke	apoplexia, garuneko odol-jario	derrame cerebral
support	sostengu	apoio
suspended	kaleratua	expulsado
swollen	hanpatua	inchada
sympathetic	gupidatsu, errukibera	comprensiva
take us to court	auzitara eramango gaitu	demandarnos
tax department	zerga-bulego, zerga-departamentu	oficina / departamento de impostos
the homeless	etxegabeak	os sen teito
threatened to report	salatzearekin mehatxatu zuen	ameazou con denunciar
tip	eskupeko	propina
tore it up	puskatu / txiki-txiki egin zuen	rompeuno / esnaquizouno
up-to-date	eguneratua	posto ao día
wouldn't release	ez ninduen askatzen	non me soltaba
yashmak	belo (musulman batzuek janzten dutena)	veo (que levan algunhas musulmás)

CROSS-CURRICULAR FOCUS
Social Changes in Britain

SOCIAL WELFARE SERVICES

Fifteen cents isn't worth much today, is it? But in the interwar years in Britain, it could save your life. Fifteen cents was the cost of a visit to the doctor. However, in those days, many working-class people couldn't afford medical treatment or even fuel to keep their homes warm in the winter. It wasn't uncommon for a family of 12 to live in a two-bedroom house where it was so cold there was ice on the inside of the windows. These were the hard realities of the life in the UK in the 1930s.

Although there was a National Health Insurance scheme, which provided benefits for unemployed and sick workers, it didn't protect workers' families, so children weren't able to receive free medical services. Medicine and doctors were a luxury and there weren't any antibiotics, so babies often died of illnesses such as pneumonia. By 1932, millions of people were unemployed so the government reduced the unemployment benefits it was giving by 10%, forcing millions of working-class people into poverty. These families had to depend on **charities** for food, clothes and education. **Workhouse** hospitals provided them with medical care.

Then, in 1942, a British economist named William Beveridge introduced a plan to help rebuild the country after World War II. His plan created a national system of benefits to protect the British people "from the **cradle** to the grave". These services included unemployment benefits, health services and education services. In order to pay for these services, every working person would pay a percentage of his/her salary to the government. In 1945, the Labour government put Beveridge's plan into action, turning Britain into a welfare state. At last, there was hope of narrowing the difference between the rich and the poor.

charities	organizaciones benéficas	organitzacions benèfiques	ongintzako erakunde(ak)	organizacións benéficas
Workhouse	(de) asilo de pobres	(d')asil de desvalguts	txiroen etxe(ko)	(de) asilo de pobres
cradle	cuna	bressol	sehaska	berce

1 Match each title to the sentences it describes. Use each title twice.

a. Living Conditions in the UK in the 1930s

b. Health Services and Unemployment Benefits before World War II

c. The British Welfare State

.... 1. Children didn't receive any free medical services.

.... 2. A family of 12 often lived in a two-bedroom house.

.... 3. William Beveridge created a national system of benefits.

.... 4. Charities provided food and clothes for the unemployed.

.... 5. The Labour government implemented Beveridge's plan.

.... 6. Many working-class homes had ice on the inside of the windows.

2 Write T (true) or F (false) next to each sentence below.

.... 1. In the 1930s in Britain, 15 cents wasn't a lot of money.

.... 2. The British working class earned a lot of money in those days.

.... 3. The National Health Insurance scheme was only for people who were working.

.... 4. In 1932, the rate of unemployment was lower than ever.

.... 5. Beveridge's plan aimed to protect the British people from birth to death.

.... 6. The objective of the welfare state was to create social equality.

William Beveridge, British economist

MARGARET THATCHER

The Growing Pains of Adrian Mole is set in the 1980s, a time of major social change in Britain. Margaret Thatcher was prime minister of the country, and introduced more changes than any other British prime minister since Winston Churchill. She became known as the "Iron Lady" because she was very determined and wouldn't compromise on her policies.

Margaret Thatcher was born in 1925 in Grantham, England. When she was 14, World War II broke out – life was very hard and people were poor. During this time, Margaret helped her parents in their small shop and also helped her father, a local politician, with his election campaigns. In 1959, after years of campaigning, she was elected Member of Parliament.

In 1970, Thatcher became Minister for Education. It was during this time that she earned a reputation for being a hard politician. She was quite pleased when she was given the nickname the "Iron Lady" – by a Russian newspaper – because she believed this showed she was a strong leader.

In 1974, Thatcher took over leadership of the Conservative Party. In May 1979, the Conservative Party won the general election, and Margaret Thatcher became prime minister. In addition to the enormous changes she made to the economy, she had to **deal with social unrest,** a miners' strike and **inner-city riots**. In 1982, she sent British warships to the Falklands. By winning the war, Britain once again felt a powerful country. Thatcher served for eleven and a half years, longer than any other British prime minister in the 20th century, but her domineering personality and her refusal to agree to a **common currency** for Europe led the Conservative Party to force her out of office. She resigned as prime minister in November 1990.

deal with	ocuparse de	ocupar-se de	(-ren) ardura izan	se ocupar de
social unrest	malestar social	malestar social	gizarte-ondoez	malestar social
inner-city riots	disturbios en los barrios céntricos pobres	disturbis en els barris cèntrics pobres	istiluak erdialdeko auzo txiroetan	disturbios nos barrios céntricos pobres
common currency	moneda única	moneda única	moneta bakar	moeda única

3 Find evidence in the text that supports the following statements about Margaret Thatcher. Write the answers in your notebook.

1. She didn't come from a wealthy background.
2. Her father was influential in getting her into politics.
3. She saw her nickname as being positive.
4. When she became prime minister, there were many problems in Britain.
5. In the end, she lost the support of her own party.

4 Complete the sentences with the words below.

politics reputation economy country refusal social change

1. The 1980s were a time of major .... in Britain.
2. The name "Iron Lady" refers to Margaret Thatcher's .... as a very determined woman.
3. Margaret was exposed to .... long before she was elected Member of Parliament.
4. During Thatcher's leadership, she made major changes to the ....
5. Thatcher's decision to send British warships to the Falklands helped the .... gain power.
6. Thatcher's .... to use the same currency as other countries in Europe led to her resignation.

MINI TASK

Search the Internet for information about Winston Churchill. What kind of prime minister was he? What important social and economic changes did he make? Write a paragraph using the information you find. Read it to the class.